# Up & Running
# with DOS 3.3

# Up & Running
# with DOS®3.3

### Michael-Alexander Beisecker

San Francisco • Paris • Düsseldorf • Soest

Acquisitions Editor: Dianne King
Series Editor: Joanne Cuthbertson
Translator: Alpnet
Editor: Tanya Kucak
Technical Review: SYBEX Technical Staff
Production Editor: Carolina Montilla
Word Processors: Winnie Kelly and Lisa Mitchell
Book Designer: Elke Hermanowski
Icon Designer: Helen Bruno
Artist: Ingrid Owen
Technical Art: Delia Brown
Desktop Publishing Production: Deborah Maizels, Charles Cowens,
    Daniel Brodnitz, Helen Bruno
Proofreader: Barbara Dahl
Cover Designer: Archer Designs

# Up & Running

Let's say that you are comfortable with your PC. You know the basic functions of word processing, spreadsheets, and database management. In short, you are a committed and eager PC user who would like to gain familiarity with several popular programs as quickly as possible. The Up & Running series of books from SYBEX has been developed for you.

*Who this book is for*

This clearly structured guide shows you in 20 steps what the product can do, how you make it work, and how soon you can achieve practical results.

*What this book provides*

Your Up & Running book thus satisfies two needs: It describes the program's capabilities, and it lets you quickly get acquainted with the program's operation. This provides valuable help for a purchase decision. You also receive a 20-step basic course that provides a solid foundation in the program—even if you're a beginner with scant prior knowledge.

The benefits are plain to see. First, you will invest in software that meets your needs, because, thanks to the appropriate Up & Running book, you will know the program's features and limitations. Second, once you purchase the product, you can skip the instruction manual and learn the basics of the program by following the 20 steps.

We have structured the Up & Running books so that the busy user spends little time studying documentation and the beginner is not burdened with unnecessary text.

A clock shows your work time for each step. This indicates how much time you can expect to spend on each step with your computer.

*Structure of the book*

Clock

Naturally, you'll need much less time if you only read through the steps rather than carrying them out at your computer. You can also save some time by scanning the short notes in the margins to find the most important sections within a step.

Three symbols are used to highlight points of special note. These symbols and their meanings are shown below:

*Symbols*

 **Action**

 **Tip**

 **Warning**

An Up & Running book cannot, of course, replace a book or manual containing advanced applications. However, you will get the information needed to put the program to practical use and to learn its basic functions.

The first step always covers software installation in relation to hardware requirements. You'll learn how to operate the program with your available hardware. Various methods for starting the program are also explained.

*Contents*

The second step introduces the program's user interface.

The remaining 18 steps demonstrate basic functions, using examples or short descriptions. You also learn about the most important commands for managing files and directories and using peripherals. The last steps cover special program features, such as customizing your system, using the built-in line editor, and additional programs provided by third parties. If information regarding recently announced program versions is available at printing time, new features are introduced to the extent possible.

*Steps 3–20*

Now you see how an Up & Running book will save you time and money.

SYBEX is very interested in your reaction to the Up & Running series. Your opinions and suggestions will help all of our readers, including yourself.

# Preface: Up & Running with DOS 3.3

This book was written primarily as a quick introduction to DOS 3.3. Nevertheless, space has been provided for several subjects that are usually treated as stepchildren in DOS manuals: batch files, device drivers, and DEBUG. It also contains many tips and applications obtained by practical experience.

Please don't simply skim through these pages; set aside the few hours necessary to completely work through this small book. Experiment with the commands and the switches that are introduced, but note the warnings and hints associated with each command. After a thorough study of this book, you will be able to configure your DOS optimally and be able to use it effectively.

—Michael-Alexander Beisecker, February 1990

# Table of Contents

Before installation, you need to make working copies, or backup copies, of your original program disks. You make backups of MS/PC-DOS 3.3 by copying the files from the 3.5" original diskette or from the two 5.25" original diskettes onto one or more diskettes (of the same size and density). Prepare backup copies of your DOS diskette(s) as follows:

*Preparing backup copies*

    DISKCOPY A: A:

to copy onto a floppy disk in the same drive, or

    DISKCOPY A: B:

to copy onto a floppy disk in drive B.

You cannot use DISKCOPY with a hard disk.

Press the Enter key following the appropriate command, and follow the prompts. You will find an exact description of the DISKCOPY command in Step 6. Entering commands is described more fully in the next step.

*Entering commands*

## Operating MS/PC-DOS with Floppy-Disk Drives

To start MS/PC-DOS, insert your backup copy of the DOS startup diskette into drive A. Now you only need to turn the computer on and DOS will boot up.

*Starting DOS*

If your computer is already on, switch it off and then on again, or press the key combination Ctrl-Alt-Del.

If the computer has two drives, insert the second DOS diskette or a diskette containing an application program into the second drive. On a single-drive system, you will need to swap the diskettes continually. For this reason, you should copy the most important system files directly on the diskettes containing your application program. Do this with the SYS command:

```
SYS B:
```

The DOS startup disk must be in drive A before invoking this command.

If you have a dual-drive system with a 5.25" and 3.5" drive, you cannot use the SYS command to copy your system files to the same type of formatted disk.

Also copy the COMMAND.COM file onto the new system disk:

```
COPY COMMAND.COM B:
```

## Installing to a Hard Disk

To install DOS onto a hard disk, the disk must already be pre-formatted and partitioned into individual partitions using the FDISK program. Normally, your PC dealer will perform these operations for you; therefore, the following instructions assume that your hard disk has been prepared appropriately.

Insert the DOS startup diskette into drive A and boot the computer (turn the computer on). After the prompt for date and time, you should receive the following display:

```
A>
```

*Changing a drive*      If **C** appears on your screen instead of **A,** then you are located on your hard disk, and not on your floppy-disk drive. You should then change to the floppy-disk drive with the following command:

```
A:
```

Now start the SYS program to copy the DOS system files onto the hard disk:

```
SYS C:
```

*Copying system files*

Next, copy the COMMAND.COM file and all drivers with the following commands:

```
COPY COMMAND.COM C:
COPY AUTOEXEC.BAT
COPY *.SYS C:
COPY *.CPI C:
```

*Copying COMMAND .COM and drivers*

The asterisk characters are *wildcards* denoting all file names with the given extensions.

If you have already created the configuration files AUTOEXEC.BAT and CONFIG.SYS, rename them before copying:

*Protecting configuration files*

```
REN AUTOEXEC.BAT *.ALT
REN CONFIG.SYS *.ALT
```

If you already have AUTOEXEC.BAT and CONFIG.SYS on your system disk, you will delete them if you add new files with the same file names. Using REN protects your existing files.

Now, change to drive C and create the DOS subdirectory there:

*Subdirectory for DOS*

```
C:
MD DOS
```

You'll find more details on the MD (make directory) command in Step 5.

*Copying DOS files*

Change into this directory and copy all files from the diskette in drive A into it:

```
CD DOS
COPY A:*.*
```

You'll find more details on the CD (check directory) command in Step 5. Note that the wildcard characters *.* allow DOS to copy all files with any extensions on drive A.

If you are using 5.25" diskettes, do not forget the files on the second diskette. To copy these files, you must remove the DOS startup diskette from drive A and insert the second DOS diskette. Then use the COPY command again:

```
COPY A:*.*
```

Remove the DOS diskette from drive A. If you renamed the configuration files, copy them under the system names:

```
COPY AUTOEXEC.ALT *.BAT
COPY CONFIG.ALT *.SYS
```

*Starting DOS*

Now you can start DOS from the hard disk by pressing the Ctrl-Alt-Del keys simultaneously.

Make sure there are no DOS diskettes in drive A before rebooting with Ctrl-Alt-Del.

# Step 2
# User Interface

MS/PC-DOS 3.3 is controlled exclusively by commands that are entered on a command line following the DOS prompt (the ready display or entry prompt by DOS). The prompt consists of the letter code of the current drive followed by a greater-than sign, as in

*Prompt*

    A>

A flashing underscore character indicates the current position of the cursor. The cursor or position indicator marks the position on the screen at which you can enter the commands. You enter commands through the keyboard.

*Cursor*

## Function Keys

You can speed up command entry by using function keys and some particular key combinations. Table 2.1 provides an overview of these keys and their functions.

| Key | Function |
|-----|----------|
| F1 | Transfers the next character from the keyboard buffer and outputs it into the command line. |
| F2*n* | Transfers all characters from the beginning of the last entry up to (but not including) the character *n* from the keyboard buffer and outputs them into the command line. |
| F3 | Transfers the entire last entry from the keyboard buffer when the cursor stands at the beginning of the line. If the cursor is located at another position, |

*Table 2.1: Standard assignment of the function keys at the DOS prompt*

| Key | Function |
|-----|----------|
| | copies all remaining characters in the keyboard buffer to the screen. |
| F4*n* | Skips over the characters in the keyboard buffer, from the beginning of the last entry up to the character *n* that you have typed in. The new contents of the keyboard buffer are not displayed in the command line. |
| F5 | Copies the text you enter after pressing F5 into the keyboard buffer. |
| F6 | Inserts an end-of-file mark (^Z). This character can also be generated by the key combination Ctrl-Z. |
| F7 | Corresponds to the key combination Ctrl-@. |
| Alt*nnn* | Displays an ASCII character on the screen. The ASCII code of the character must be entered as *nnn* on the number pad. |
| Ctrl-C | Interrupts a batch file and many DOS commands. |
| Ctrl-P | Directs the screen output to the printer. |
| Ctrl-S | Stops screen output. |
| Ctrl-Z | Generates an end-of-file character. |
| Ctrl-Alt-Del | "Warm boots" the processor. |
| ← | Moves the cursor one space to the left and deletes the previous character. |
| → | Moves the cursor one space to the right. In this case, the next character is transferred from the keyboard buffer and displayed. |

*Table 2.1: Standard assignment of the function keys at the DOS prompt (cont.)*

| Key | Function |
|-----|----------|
| Ins | Toggles between insert and typeover mode. |
| Enter | Terminates command entry. The specified command is now executed if it does not contain an error. Every entry is stored in the keyboard buffer (even faulty entries). |
| Del | Erases the characters to the left of the cursor. |
| Esc | Interrupts an entry without executing the command. A backslash (\) appears on the screen. You can begin inserting a new command again after this character, or you can display a new line by pressing the Enter key. If you press the Enter key following the backslash, the command will not be executed and you will not receive an error message. |

*Table 2.1: Standard assignment of the function keys at the DOS prompt (cont.)*

## Entering Commands

You enter commands such as MD or COPY in Step 1 immediately following the prompt. It does not matter to DOS whether you enter commands in uppercase or lowercase letters. Additional specifications, in the form of option switches, can follow most commands. Switches differ from other input options such as drive specifications, path specifications, and file names: a switch always begins with a forward slash. In the following example, the CHKDSK command is entered along with the /F switch:

*Option switches*

```
CHKDSK D: /F
```

D:, which is also a parameter, transmits the name of the drive—in this case, the name of the hard disk D. The command is not executed until you press the Enter key. Before pressing Enter, you can edit the command using the cursor keys and the keys specified in Table 2.1.

*F3 key*

If you need to execute the same command repeatedly, simply press the F3 key. The last command entered then appears, and you can edit it as desired. You will be introduced to expanded functions in the next section.

## Internal and External Commands

*System files*

DOS consists of a collection of files. In addition to the system files IBMBIO.COM and IBMDOS.COM with PC-DOS, or IO.SYS and MSDOS.SYS with MS-DOS, the command interpreter COMMAND.COM is part of the core of the operating system. The machine-language routines for execution of the *internal commands* are filed in the command interpreter. These are also called *resident commands,* since they are loaded with the command interpreter into the main memory when the system is booted, and they remain there.

*Internal commands*

On the other hand, programs that can be stored in special files in a chosen directory are called *external commands.* In contrast to internal commands, external commands will not be found if the program files are not located in the current directory or if you have not provided information about the location of the files. Either change to the drive and directory where the program files are located, or specify the respective drive and directory before the command:

```
C:\DOS\CHKDSK D:
```

To avoid having to repeat the entire path specification before every command, you can use the PATH command to specify a list of directories that DOS should search to find an external command file if it is not located in the current directory. You will learn how to make these settings in Step 15. Table 2.2 lists all internal and external DOS commands.

| *Internal Commands* | *External Commands* |
| --- | --- |
| BREAK | APPEND |
| CD/CHDIR | ASSIGN |
| CHCP | ATTRIB |
| CLS | BACKUP |
| COPY | CHKDSK |
| CTTY | COMMAND |
| DATE | COMP |
| DEL | DEBUG |
| DIR | DISKCOMP |
| ECHO | DISKCOPY |
| ERASE | EDLIN |
| EXIT | EXE2BIN |
| FOR | FASTOPEN |
| GOTO | FC |
| IF | FDISK |
| MD/MKDIR | FIND |
| PATH | FORMAT |
| PAUSE | GRAFTABL |
| PROMPT | GRAPHICS |
| RD/RMDIR | JOIN |
| REM | KEYB |
| REN/RENAME | LABEL |
| SET | MODE |
| SHIFT | MORE |
| TIME | NLSFUNC |
| TYPE | PRINT |
| VER | RECOVER |
| VERIFY | REPLACE |
| VOL | RESTORE |
| | SELECT |
| | SHARE |

*Table 2.2: Internal and external commands*

| Internal Commands | External Commands |
|---|---|
| | SORT |
| | SUBST |
| | SYS |
| | TREE |
| | XCOPY |

*Table 2.2: Internal and external commands (cont.)*

# Initial Commands

After the computer has been booted, the set date will normally be displayed in the following format:

```
Current date is Fri 02-09-1990
Enter new date (mm-dd-yy):
```

Here *mm, dd,* and *yy* represent the month, day, and year. If your computer does not have a built-in clock, the standard default 01-01-1980 is displayed. It is important that you insert the correct current date. The correct time and date setting is necessary for the proper operation of many application programs (invoicing, bookkeeping, schedule management, and so on).

*Standard default*

Since the system stamps every file with the time and date when it was created or last modified, the date and time can be useful for documentation purposes and can be helpful in tracking down errors in a program package. If you own a PC with a built-in clock, this clock will display the current date, and you need only press the Enter key to confirm it.

The date format depends on the setting of the COUNTRY command in the CONFIG.SYS file. If this file does not exist (or if this command is not contained in the file), the default date will be the American default as indicated above. For example, you can display this German default by setting the COUNTRY command:

*Date format*

```
Current date is Fri 9.02.1990
Enter new date (dd.mm.yy):
```

The current time is displayed after the date:

```
Current time is 2:23:12.45p
Enter new time:
```

Computers without built-in clocks display 0:00:00.00 as the default time. In this case, the correct time needs to be specified for the reasons listed above. If your PC displays the correct time, just press the Enter key.

The commands DATE and TIME are executed by the AUTOEXEC.BAT file when you boot the system. (*Note*: If your system disk has no AUTOEXEC.BAT file, DOS will prompt you for the date and time. If you have an AUTOEXEC.BAT file, it must contain the DATE and TIME commands for DOS to issue the date and time prompts.)

You can display system date and the system time at any time, however, by entering the commands at the DOS prompt. The same information will be displayed as during the booting of the computer. If you wish to change the displayed date, simply type in the new date directly following the command:

*DATE*
*command*

```
DATE 02-29-1990
```

In this case, an incorrect date was specified and an error message appears:

*Error*

```
Invalid date
Enter new date (mm-dd-yy):
```

If you enter an incorrect time, a similar message will appear. Like the date, the current time can be displayed at any time at the DOS prompt:

*TIME*
*command*

```
TIME
```

To display the current time, simply enter the command without parameters. Press Enter once after displaying the date to return to the DOS prompt.

Often, the AUTOEXEC.BAT file will also contain the command VER. This is activated with each boot of the computer and displays the installed DOS version:

**IBM Personal Computer DOS-Version 3.3**

You can also call up this internal command from any DOS prompt without any parameters:

**VER**

Now you have an entire screen filled with time, date, and version numbers and you can test the CLS command. CLS is the abbreviation for *clear screen,* which means "erase the screen." Your PC executes this instruction immediately, and the screen contents are erased:

**CLS**

Your screen will not be completely empty after erasing, since the DOS prompt and the cursor appear at the upper left corner of the screen. Remember the CLS command when you are taught the programming of batch files in Step 14. In addition to its use at the DOS prompt, this command is also convenient for erasing the screen between messages from batch files.

*VER command*

*DOS version*

*CLS command*

*Erase screen*

*CLS in batch files*

# Step 4
# Formatting Diskettes

As a rule, you must initialize new diskettes before you can use them in your system to store data. You use the external command FORMAT to initialize diskettes and to reformat old, previously used diskettes. The formatting procedure not only erases old data on used diskettes, but also locates bad sectors and labels these so that they cannot be used for data storage.

*FORMAT command*

The FORMAT command can perform various types of disk formatting if your system contains the required disk drives (1.2Mb, 5.25" and 1.44Mb, 3.5"). The possible FORMAT settings are as follows:

    [d:path] FORMAT dl: [/S][/1][/4][/8][/V]
       [/B][N:xx][T:yy]

*Syntax of FORMAT*

*d:path* specifies the drive and path of the command file if this is not found in the current directory.

*dl:* is the drive containing the diskette that is to be formatted.

/S copies the operating-system files.

/1 formats the disk as a single-sided disk.

/4 formats a 360Kb disk in a 1.2Mb drive.

/8 formats a disk with eight instead of nine sectors per track.

/V prompts for a volume name (a name for the disk) after formatting.

/B formats a disk with eight sectors per track and reserves space for the operating-system files without copying them.

/N:*xx* formats a disk with *xx* sectors per track. You can use the values from Table 4.1 for this.

/T:*yy* formats a disk with *yy* tracks. You can use the values from Table 4.1 for this.

*Partition-ing a disk*

During formatting, a disk is divided into tracks (concentric rings). The number of tracks depends on the size of the disk and its storage capacity. As a rule, each disk side contains 40 or 80 tracks, which are in turn divided into 9, 15, or 18 sectors. Table 4.1 lists common disk formats and the tracks and sectors associated with these formats. These values are necessary for the correct specification of the /N and /T parameters.

*Parameters for /N and /T*

| Disk Format (all double-sided) | 5.25" double density (DS/DD) | 5.25" high density (DS/HD) | 3.5" double density (DS/DD) | 3.5" high density (DS/HD) |
|---|---|---|---|---|
| Tracks per Inch (tpi) | 48 | 96 | 135 | 135 |
| Track Number | 40 | 80 | 80 | 80 |
| Sectors per Track | 9 | 15 | 9 | 18 |
| Bytes per Sector | 512 | 512 | 512 | 512 |
| Sector Number | 720 | 2400 | 1440 | 2880 |
| Storage Capacity | 360Kb | 1.2Mb | 720Kb | 1.4Mb |

*Table 4.1: Storage organization of the more common disk formats*

*Formatting diskettes*

Formatting a disk in drive A is probably the most frequent use of the FORMAT command. The following entry is all that is required for this:

```
FORMAT A:
```

The FORMAT program determines the format the disk will have, based on the drive type. In a 5.25" high-capacity drive, disks are automatically formatted as 1.2Mb diskettes; a 5.25" double-density drive can format up to 360Kb on a diskette. Using switches, however, you can format a 360Kb diskette in a 1.2Mb drive:

*360Kb diskette in 1.2Mb drive*

```
FORMAT A: /4
```

You can even format a diskette for 180Kb in a 1.2Mb drive:

```
FORMAT A: /4 /1
```

The switches /N and /T also allow you to format 3.5" diskettes with double density (720Kb) in a high-capacity, 1.44Mb diskette drive:

*720Kb diskette in 1.44Mb drive*

```
FORMAT A: /N:9 /T:80
```

You can also format your hard disk with FORMAT. To prepare the disk, divide it into individual areas (partitions) with the FDISK command if this has not been done previously. An expanded partition can be further partitioned into logical drives. Each of these logical drives and the primary partition must be formatted individually with FORMAT. Do not use this command when data is already on the hard disk, however, since all data would be lost.

*Formatting hard disks*

To protect against unintentionally formatting the hard disk, FORMAT either prompts for the volume label (the name) of the hard disk or gives the following warning:

*Naming the hard disk*

```
FORMAT C:
WARNING! All data on the non-removable
disk E: will be lost!
Proceed with format (Y/N)?
```

If you confirm this message with Y (Yes), FORMAT immediately begins to format your hard disk. All data on this disk are then lost, so be very careful with this command!

RAM disks and drives that have received a new drive identifier through ASSIGN cannot be formatted by FORMAT.

## Naming a Diskette or Hard Disk

*LABEL*
*command*

For quick identification of the contents of a diskette or hard disk, you can give it a name during formatting (using /V). You can also name the disk using the LABEL command.

LABEL is easy to use. The following example shows how the disk in drive A receives the name LETTERS:

```
LABEL A:LETTERS
```

The disk name, which is also called the volume identifier or label, cannot contain the following characters:

```
* ? / \ | . , ; : + = < > [ ] ( ) @ ^ .
```

If you do not specify a name, LABEL displays the current volume identifier and requests a name:

```
LABEL D:
Volume in drive D is HONEY

Volume label (11 characters, ENTER for
none)_
```

*Erasing*
*labels*

This volume already has a name. If you press the Enter key at this point, DOS inquires whether you wish to erase the label:

```
Delete current volume label (Y/N)?
```

The name is retained if you enter N.

## Displaying the Label

The name you give to a volume with the FORMAT or LABEL command is displayed every time you list the contents of a directory with the DIR command. Listing a directory, however, takes a long time compared to simply listing the name of a volume label. For this reason, DOS contains the VOL command, which displays the volume identifier immediately.

*VOL*
*command*

Entering VOL without parameters displays the label of the volume in the current drive:

```
VOL
Volume in drive D: is HONEY
```

However, it can also specify which drive will be queried:

```
VOL A:
Volume in drive A: has no label
```

## Checking Floppy Disks and Hard Disks

The CHKDSK command checks your floppy disk or hard disk for errors in the file entries. It also gives a status report on the number of stored data files and the amount of storage space still available on the storage disk and in the main memory. CHKDSK does provide a function for eliminating errors, but you should also have programs such as Norton Utilities or Disk Technician at your disposal.

*CHKDSK*
*command*

The settings for CHKDSK are as follows:

*Syntax of*
*CHKDSK*

```
[d:path] CHKDSK [d1:path1][filespec][/F]
    [/V]
```

*d:path* specifies the drive and the path of the command file.

*dl*: specifies the drive being checked.

*filespec* specifies the optional drive and path, along with the file name and extension of the file that is to be investigated for fragmentation. The wildcard characters * and ? are permitted.

**/F** eliminates errors found on the diskette or hard disk.

**/V** displays all files with their path specifications.

Enter CHKDSK without any options to check the current drive:

```
CHKDSK
```

The output of this command appears as follows:

```
Disk HONEY created 08-12-1988 5:13p

26128384 bytes total disk space
0        bytes in 1 hidden file
81920    bytes in 29 directories
25677824 bytes in 1236 user files
368640   bytes available on disk

654336   total bytes memory
575744   bytes free
```

*Directories occupy memory space*

The total disk space is reported in the second line. This example refers to a 20Mb hard disk that contains no system files, or a 20Mb logical drive in an expanded partition. There are no hidden files. *Hidden files* are system files that an application program has added as part of a copyright protection. This report shows that directories occupy memory space. The 29 directories in this example occupy nearly 80Kb. The last two lines display the total amount of main memory in bytes and the number of bytes currently available.

If a CHKDSK command finds errors in the file allocation table (FAT), you will need to execute it again to eliminate the errors, this time using the /F option:

```
CHKDSK /F
```

After you have answered Y to eliminate errors found, CHKDSK saves lost and incorrectly allocated sectors of defective files into consecutively numbered files with the labels FILE0000.CHK, FILE0001.CHK, FILE0002.CHK, and so on. You can use these error files only if the original files were text files. If this is the case, you can recover a portion of the original file in this manner.

One variation of the CHKDSK command displays whether files are fragmented:

```
D>CHKDSK *.*

Volume HONEY created 08-12-1988, 5:13p

26128384 bytes total disk space
0        bytes in 1 hidden files
81920    bytes in 29 directories
25681920 bytes in 1238 user files
364544   bytes available on disk

645336   bytes total memory
177680   bytes free

D:\ABB05_3.SCR
Contains 2 non-contiguous blocks.
```

In this example, CHKDSK found that the \ABB05_3.SCR file on drive D is fragmented and contains two noncontiguous blocks.

*Eliminating*
*fragmentation*

If there is a great deal of fragmentation on a hard disk, you should use a utility such as Disk Optimizer to optimize the speed at which your hard drive is accessed. You might wish to back up the hard disk, reformat, and then restore the files to the hard disk. This, however, takes quite a bit of time.

# Step 5
# File Management

DOS allows you to partition hard disks and diskettes into directories. The directory structure is laid out hierarchically in the form of a tree (see Figure 5.1). The root of this tree (at the top) forms the root or main directory. Subdirectories branch off of this root directory, which in turn can have subdirectories branch off from them. Each directory, then, can contain subdirectories and files.

## Display Directory Contents

You can display the file and directory entries with the DIR command. The file name, the file extension, and the date and time of creation or modification of the file are displayed. Without parameters, DIR displays all files in the current directory:

```
DIR
```

*DIR
command*

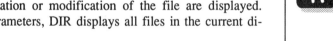

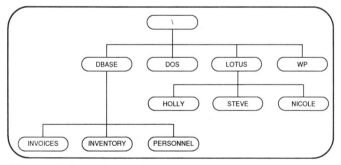

*Figure 5.1: Example of a directory structure*

You also can read files from other directories:

```
DIR D:/WORD5/DOCS
```

*Tabular format*

For reviewing, you can have the directory contents listed in table format by using the /W switch:

```
DIR D:\WORD5\DOCS /W
```

Using this option, the file entries are listed in five adjoining columns without their size, date, and time stamps.

*Display by page*

Larger directory indexes can best be displayed using the /P switch. The list is then halted after each screen page, and you can examine it at your leisure:

```
DIR D:\WORD5\DOCS /P
```

Continue the display by pressing any key.

The DIR lists do not contain any hidden files. To display these files, you must first cancel the hidden attribute using Norton Utilities, PC Tools Deluxe, or a similar program.

## Changing File Attributes

*ATTRIB command*

The ATTRIB command can control the way some DOS commands affect a file by changing the file's attributes. For example, by selecting the appropriate file attributes, you can prevent a file from being accidentally erased or overwritten.

*Read-only (R) Archive (A)*

Each file can be assigned read-only (R) and archive (A) attributes with ATTRIB. The following command protects the specified files from being overwritten by assigning them the read-only attribute:

```
ATTRIB +R DIPLOM??.TXT
```

*Note*: The ? wildcard characters denote any single character in the file name. In this example, all files beginning with DIPLOM and any other two characters and ending with the .TXT extension will be protected.

Now these files cannot be modified or deleted. If you receive a diskette with read-only files, you can cancel the protection by using ATTRIB:

```
ATTRIB -R A:\ /S
```

You use the /S switch to set or remove the attributes of all files in a subdirectory simultaneously. You cannot cancel a physical write-protector, such as a sticker or a slide, by this command.

*Files in subdirectories*

The archive attribute of a file is set automatically by DOS when the file is modified. Several DOS commands (such as XCOPY or BACKUP) can be set to copy only data with a set archive attribute and remove it automatically after each copy operation. The following examples show how all files in subdirectory \PASCAL are assigned the archive attribute:

```
ATTRIB +A D:\PASCAL\*.*
```

## Creating a Directory

MD (also called MKDIR) creates a new subdirectory from the root directory or from a subdirectory on the current drive or a different drive. The new directory is empty but is usable immediately.

*MD/ MKDIR command*

The simplest use of this command is the creation of a subdirectory branching off the current directory:

*Subdirectory*

```
MD DOS
```

If you are currently in the root directory, you have now created the directory \DOS. If you are located in the directory \WORD\DOCS, then you have now created the directory \WORD\DOCS\DOS.

MD can create directories on any connected drives. The following command creates the directory \EXAMPLE on drive E:

    MD E:\EXAMPLE

*Parent directory*

The MD command cannot create a directory if the directory name matches the name of a file in the parent directory. DOS will also display the error message

*Error*

    Directory cannot be created

when a directory already contains the maximum number of file entries.

## Changing a Directory

*CD/ CHDIR command*

CD (or CHDIR) allows you to change directories within a drive. You can use this command without parameters to display the current drive and directory for orientation purposes.

    CD
    C:\DOS

## Deleting a Directory

*RD/ RMDIR command*

RD (also called RMDIR) deletes a specified empty subdirectory on the current drive or on a different drive. You should immediately delete any unnecessary subdirectories, since they occupy memory space. It is also easier to manage the directory structure if you delete unnecessary subdirectories.

The following command deletes the \INVOICE\PURCHASE directory from the current drive:

```
RD \INVOICE\PURCHASE
```

You delete a directory on a different drive by adding the drive specification to the directory name:

```
RD D:\OLDDATA
```

If \OLDDATA still contains file entries, an error message is displayed:

```
Invalid path, not directory
or directory not empty
```

*Error*

A directory is not empty if it contains a subdirectory, even if it does not contain any files!

## Displaying a Directory Structure

The TREE command displays all directories on a drive and, if desired, all files contained in the directory. The contents are displayed in list format (see Figure 5.2):

*TREE command*

```
TREE
```

Including the /F switch causes all files in all subdirectories to be displayed as well (see Figure 5.3). This display, however, is rather cumbersome with larger directories.

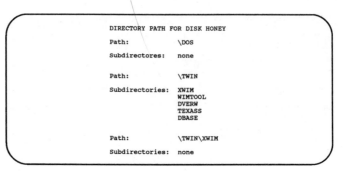

```
          DIRECTORY PATH FOR DISK HONEY

          Path:            \DOS

          Subdirectores:   none


          Path:            \TWIN

          Subdirectories:  XWIM
                           WIMTOOL
                           DVERW
                           TEXASS
                           DBASE


          Path:            \TWIN\XWIM

          Subdirectories:  none
```

*Figure 5.2: Output of the TREE command*

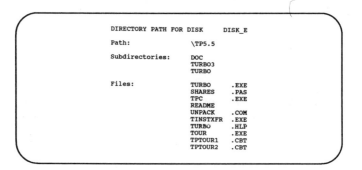

```
          DIRECTORY PATH FOR DISK     DISK_E

          Path:            \TP5.5

          Subdirectories:  DOC
                           TURBO3
                           TURBO

          Files:           TURBO      .EXE
                           SHARES     .PAS
                           TPC        .EXE
                           README
                           UNPACK     .COM
                           TINSTXFR   .EXE
                           TURBO      .HLP
                           TOUR       .EXE
                           TPTOUR1    .CBT
                           TPTOUR2    .CBT
```

*Figure 5.3: Output of the TREE command with switch /F*

# Copying Files

There are seven commands for copying files in DOS: SYS, COPY, XCOPY, DISKCOPY, REPLACE, BACKUP, and RESTORE. You can check the prepared copies with the commands COMP and DISKCOMP.

## Copying System Files

The SYS command copies the operating-system files to the specified drive (IO.SYS and MSDOS.SYS for MS-DOS, and IBMBIO.COM and IBMDOS.COM for PC-DOS); SYS does not copy COMMAND.COM and the other DOS program files. By doing this, the SYS command transforms a data disk into a system disk or updates the DOS located on a hard disk.

*System files*

*SYS command*

The syntax of the SYS command is as follows:

    [d:path] SYS targetdrive:

*Syntax of SYS*

A floppy disk must be completely blank before system files are transferred to it with the SYS command, since the system files must be the first loaded on it. To transfer the system to the hard disk, insert a system disk in drive A and change to this drive before entering the command. The following command then copies the system files from the A drive to the hard disk:

*Transfer-ring the system to the hard disk*

    SYS C:

You can encounter the same problem of not being able to transfer the system files if there are already system files (of a previous version, for instance) on the hard disk. The system files must reside on a specific place on the disk.

*Transfer-ring the system to a floppy disk*

Of course, you can also copy the system from drive A to a floppy disk in drive B:

```
SYS B:
```

Note that the format command's /S option also transfers system files after the format operation.

## Copying Selected Files

*COPY command*

The COPY command is frequently used for copying individual files. You can also use this command to create files that will access peripheral devices or to chain files. The COPY command has three different command formats for these functions.

*Copying files*

The first format permits individual or multiple files to be copied to a chosen directory on a connected drive:

```
COPY  C:\WORD\1989*.TXT  A:\1989
```

The files remain stored in the original directory as well as in the new location. This means that they have been duplicated and require twice the disk storage space. Copies of write-protected files are not automatically protected by COPY. The read-only attribute therefore must be reset with ATTRIB.

*Creating files*

The second format permits you to create small files without an editor:

```
COPY CON INFO.DAT
This sentence has been written into the
file INFO.DAT with COPY CON. <Ctrl><Z>
```

Any information that is input through the keyboard (console) after calling up the COPY command is copied into the file INFO.DAT—that is, is recorded there. The key combination Ctrl-Z ends the file.

The third format of the COPY command chains files. You can connect ASCII files in series and store them as one large file:

```
COPY 1989FIRM.TXT+19890FFC.TXT
     +1989HOUS.TXT TAXES89.TXT
```

In addition to file name and path specifications, you can add the following switches to the COPY command:

**/A** (before the source file name) causes the file to be input without the first Ctrl-Z character (end-of-file character) and to be treated as an ASCII file. This switch is preset in the chaining function. If you enter it before the name of the target file, a Ctrl-Z character is written at the end of the new file.

**/B** is preset in the file duplication function. Before the source file name, it causes files to be copied completely, including the terminating end-of-file marker. When you specify /B after the target file, it suppresses the Ctrl-Z character at the end of the file.

**/V** switches on the VERIFY mode for the duration of the command.

Thus, the formats of COPY are as follows:

```
COPY [/A][/B]source[/A][/B][target][/A]
     [/B][/V]
```

```
COPY [/A][/B]source1+source2[/A]
     [/B]+...[target][/A][/B][/V]
```

## Copying Groups of Files

XCOPY is an extension of the COPY command. XCOPY first reads as many files as possible into a buffer that is the size of the available memory, and then downloads the contents of this buffer. The following example shows how all text files (that is, all files with the extension .TXT) from the WORD directory can be saved:

**XCOPY C:\WORD\*.TXT A:**

*Files in subdirectories*

You can copy corresponding files in subdirectories with the /S switch:

**XCOPY C:\*.TXT /S**

Since the root directory has been specified here, all files on the hard disk that have a .TXT extension will be copied. If two files from different directories have the same name, however, the file copied last will overwrite the previous file!

You can combine various switches to select only particular files. Please note that the /E and /S switches must be placed together:

/A copies only files with the archive attribute set (see Step 5).

/D:*mm-dd-yy* copies only files that were created or modified on or after the specified date.

/E automatically creates the necessary subdirectories on the target drive, even if the subdirectories are empty. (The /S option does the same thing, but doesn't create empty directories.)

/M copies files with a set archive attribute and then resets the attribute.

/P causes a prompt to be displayed before copying.

/S copies all specified files in the subdirectories of the current directory as well as in the current directory.

/V sets the VERIFY mode on.

/W waits for a floppy disk before searching for the data to be copied.

To summarize, the format of the XCOPY command is as follows:

```
[d:path] XCOPY filespec1 [filespec2][/A]
[/D:mm-dd-yy][/E][/M][/P][/S][/V][/W]
```
*Syntax of*
*XCOPY*

## Copying a Floppy Disk

You should use DISKCOPY whenever you wish to copy an entire floppy disk. DISKCOPY produces an exact copy of the source disk. Thus, a copy of a system disk is always a system disk. Also, you can only use DISKCOPY with one size of disk; you cannot copy the contents of a 360Kb disk to a 1.2Mb disk, for instance, using DISKCOPY.

*DISKCOPY*
*command*

```
[d:path] DISKCOPY [sourcedrive:]
[targetdrive:][/1]
```
*Syntax of*
*DISKCOPY*

The /1 switch lets you copy only one side of the source diskette.

During the copy procedure, all files on the target disk are overwritten. An unformatted target disk is formatted during the copy procedure. DISKCOPY must, therefore, have access to the FORMAT program.

To copy a disk in drive A to a disk in drive B, enter the following:

*Copying*
*from A*
*to B*

```
DISKCOPY A: B:
```

If you have only one drive, specify this drive as both source drive and target drive:

*Copying*
*with a*
*single*
*drive*

```
DISKCOPY A: A:
```

You will be prompted to change disks. To protect your original disk from being accidentally overwritten, write-protect it (use the adhesive sticker on 5.25-inch disks or the slide on 3.5-inch disks).

A hard disk cannot be copied with DISKCOPY, and a floppy disk can only be reproduced in the format of the original disk. For example, DISKCOPY cannot copy a 3.5-inch disk onto a 5.25-inch disk.

*Errors*

If DISKCOPY finds an error on the source disk or target disk during copy, it will indicate the location—the drive, side, and track—where the error is found. Try the procedure again using another target diskette, or check to be sure that you are not trying to copy a copy-protected disk.

*Copy protection*

## Updating Software

*REPLACE command*

The REPLACE command is an expanded version of the COPY command. It is used primarily for updating DOS or application programs, updating single files, or selectively backing up files.

*Updating DOS*

The following example shows how DOS files in the DOS subdirectory are replaced by files of a newer version:

```
REPLACE A:*.* C:\DOS
```

Be careful not to confuse the source and target. You must always specify first where the new files are coming from and then where they are to be copied, otherwise REPLACE will copy the old files over the new files.

*Syntax of REPLACE*

```
[d:path] REPLACE sourcefile[targetdrive:]
     [/A] [/P] [/R] [/S] [/W]
```

Like COPY and XCOPY, REPLACE recognizes several switches:

**/A** copies all files on the source disk that don't exist on the target.

**/P** causes a prompt to be displayed before copying each file.

**/R** replaces read-only files in the target drive. Be careful using this switch!

**/S** replaces all files on the target drive with those having identical file names on the source.

**/W** waits for a disk to be inserted into the target drive before REPLACE replaces the files there.

Experiment with the various switches. Be sure to back up your files before doing this!

## Backing Up Data

BACKUP makes a backup of the data on your hard disk. This command is better than COPY and XCOPY for backing up files, since COPY and XCOPY cannot back up files that are larger than the storage space on a disk. BACKUP, on the other hand, can distribute the contents of large files across several floppy disks if necessary. BACKUP prompts for a new disk as one is needed.

*BACKUP command*

For safety, you should set VERIFY to ON before initiating the BACKUP command. Perform backups daily, weekly, and monthly on separate backup disks. A corrupt application program or a virus might prevent you from recognizing major errors in your data for a long time.

*Backing up an entire hard disk*

The following example shows how all files on hard disk D can be saved on diskettes:

**BACKUP   D:\*.*   A: /S**

*Backing up a single directory*

In BACKUP, just as in other copy commands, the /S switch backs up the files in all subdirectories. You can also back up a single directory if you do not need it at the moment and want to remove it from the hard disk to create space:

**BACKUP   C:\ADVISOR\*.TXT   A:**

The file FORMAT.EXE must be located in the same directory as BACKUP, since the backup diskettes might also need to be formatted. Backup disks are always formatted according to the capacity of the drive. BACKUP will not, for example, format a 360Kb disk to 360Kb in a 1.2Mb drive.

*Syntax of BACKUP*

**[d:path] BACKUP sourcedrive:[filespec]**
    **targetdrive:[/S][/M][/A][/D:mm-dd-yy]**
    **[/T:hh:mm:ss][/F][/L[:logfilespec]]**

During backup, all files on the backup disk are deleted. You can prevent this by using the /A switch. You can also use other switches to control the copying process:

/S backs up all subdirectories of the current directory.

/M backs up modified files—that is, files with a set archive attribute.

/A stores new files on the target disk without overwriting old files on the disk.

/D:*mm-dd-yy* copies only those files that were created or modified on or after the specified date.

/T:*hh:mm:ss* backs up all files that were created or modified at or after the specified time.

/F formats the target disk if it has not been previously

formatted.

**/L:***logfilespec* produces a log file. If you do not specify a file name, a file called BACKUP.LOG is created.

## Restoring Data

RESTORE replaces the files saved with BACKUP to the directory on the hard disk from which they originated. This
process is the reverse of BACKUP; you must therefore know
which directories and files were backed up by BACKUP.
Look back at the examples for the BACKUP command. The
following RESTORE commands are the reverse of those
BACKUP commands:

*RESTORE*
*command*

```
RESTORE  A:  D:\*.* /S
RESTORE  A:  C:\ADVISOR\*.TXT
```

RESTORE processes the disks in the exact sequence in which
they were saved by BACKUP. If you do not follow this sequence, RESTORE displays an error message. If you lose
a backup disk or one of these disks is damaged, you cannot
restore any disks following the bad or missing disk with
RESTORE!

```
[d:path] RESTORE sourcedrive:
   targetdrive: [filespec] [/P]
   [/A:mm-dd-yy][/B:mm-dd-yy]
   [/E:hh:mm:ss][/L:hh:mm:ss][/M][/N]
```

*Syntax of*
*RESTORE*

The RESTORE command also recognizes several switches:

**/P** prompts whether to overwrite files that have been
modified on the target drive.

**/A:***mm-dd-yy* copies backup files that were modified

on or *after* the specified date.

/B:*mm-dd-yy* copies backup files that were modified
on or *before* the specified date.

/E:*hh:mm:ss* copies backup files that were modified
before (*earlier* than) the specified time.

/L:*hh:mm:ss* copies backup files that were modified
after (*later* than) the specified time.

/M compares the files on the source and target drives,
and copies backup files that no longer exist on the
target drive or that have been modified.

/N recopies backup files that no longer exist on the
target drive.

## Checking Copied Files

*COMP
command*

Use the COMP command to compare copied files against
original files. This command compares the contents of two or
more files that can be found in different directories and
drives. Data files or program files can be compared:

```
COMP  C:\WORD\REPORT.TXT  A:\REPORT.TXT
```

If COMP finds differences, the command displays these in
the form of hexadecimal numbers. The typical DOS user will
only be able to tell from the COMP's output whether the files
being compared are identical (no errors occur) or dissimilar
(errors occur). If you have mastered the hexadecimal system,
you will be able to identify the discrepancies.

```
[d:path] COMP [d1:path1 filespec1]
    [d2:path2 filespec2]
```

*Syntax of
COMP*

# Checking Floppy Disk Copies

DISKCOMP compares floppy disks and checks them for readability. The most frequent use of this command is for checking a copy made with DISKCOPY:

*DISKCOMP command*

        DISKCOMP   A:   B:

You can also use this command if you have only a single disk drive or two disk drives with different formats. In this case, enter the same drive letter twice:

        DISKCOMP   A:   A:

You will have to change your disk several times, as DISKCOMP prompts you. DISKCOMP compares the sectors rather than the files of the disk. When comparing copies made with COPY or XCOPY, the program will frequently display error messages; the sequence of files on a disk copied with COPY or XCOPY generally deviates from their sequence on the original.

> [*d:path*] DISKCOMP [*d1*:[*d2*:]] [/1] [/8]

You can specify two switches for DISKCOMP, but these are rarely necessary:

*Syntax of DISKCOMP*

/1 compares only the first side of each diskette, regardless of their formatting.

/8 compares only the first 8 sectors of each track, regardless of the formatting of the disks. This applies to disks with 8, 9, and 15 sectors per track.

The RENAME command gives files a new name as long as no other file or subdirectory in the directory has been assigned that particular name. The abbreviation of the command is REN.

*RENAME command*

**REN[AME]  [d:path]oldname newname**

*Syntax of RENAME*

The following example renames the program CHKDSK.EXE:

**REN  CHKDSK.EXE  TESTDISK.EXE**

Using RENAME, you can abbreviate names or standardize file names for documentation.

*Redefining or abbreviating DOS commands*

If the specified file does not exist or if another file already exists with the desired new name, you will receive the following error message:

**Duplicate file name or file not found**

*Error*

After renaming, the file has a new name but is still found in the original directory. The REN command merely changes the name of the file in the file allocation table.

The RENAME command also recognizes wildcard characters, enabling you to change several file names at once:

*Multiple files*

**REN  D:\PASCAL\*.TST  *.PAS**

In this example, files with the extension .TST (for test) are renamed with the extension .PAS (pascal source code).

Unfortunately, the RENAME command cannot rename a directory, even though DOS directory management is similar to DOS file management. To rename a directory, you can use the following batch file, NEWNAME.BAT:

*Rename*
*directory*

```
REM   NEWNAME.BAT
REM   NEWNAME   [D:]\directory.old
   [D:]\directory.new
MD   %2
COPY   %1\*.*   %2
DEL   %1
RD   %1
```

If you have not yet worked with batch files, it would be better to wait to create or use NEWNAME.BAT until you have reached Step 14.

The contents of a file can be output to the screen or to the printer. The TYPE command is used to display text files on the screen.

Certain key combinations or the PRINT command will output data to the printer. PRINT is memory-resident; it prints out text files and special print files while you are working with DOS or with an application program.

## Output to the Screen

You can display the contents of an ASCII file with the TYPE command. To do this, give the name of the desired file (without wildcards such as * or ?) as a parameter following the command:

*TYPE command*

```
TYPE EXAMPLE.ASC
```

Although the file contents are displayed on the screen, longer files are almost impossible to read since they scroll down the screen without pausing. You can interrupt the display with the key combination Ctrl-S. Press any key to restart the display.

```
TYPE filespec
```

Displaying a page at a time can be accomplished more easily and efficiently by using the MORE filter:

*Syntax of TYPE*
*Display by page*

```
TYPE   EXAMPLE.ASC | MORE
```

Binary, SYS, EXE, and COM files should not be displayed with the TYPE command, since this could cause the computer to lock up or to output unintelligible graphic characters and beep. If the computer locks up, briefly switch it off and then back on. You can also restart DOS by pressing the key combination Ctrl-Alt-Del.

## Output to the Printer

Except for the keyboard and screen, the printer is the most important of the peripheral devices, since it can print the contents of files and can document the system status. You can output the current screen contents to the printer by pressing the Shift-PrtSc key combination. This procedure will only function in the text mode with IBM-compatible dot-matrix printers, and it is often limited to the text characters in the ASCII code set.

To print the graphic characters as well, you must previously start the GRAFTABL program:

*GRAFTABL*
*command*

    **GRAFTABL**

The GRAFTABL command also allows you to specify the character set:

*Syntax of*
*GRAFTABL*

    **[d:path] GRAFTABL [437|860|863|865|**
       **/STATUS]**

The /STATUS switch tells you which character set is current.

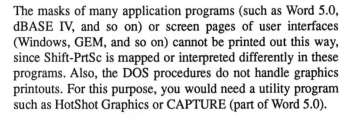

The masks of many application programs (such as Word 5.0, dBASE IV, and so on) or screen pages of user interfaces (Windows, GEM, and so on) cannot be printed out this way, since Shift-PrtSc is mapped or interpreted differently in these programs. Also, the DOS procedures do not handle graphics printouts. For this purpose, you would need a utility program such as HotShot Graphics or CAPTURE (part of Word 5.0).

*Switching*
*the printer*
*on and off*

At the DOS level, you can switch the printer on or off at any time by pressing the key combination Ctrl-P. This also prints out all screen outputs with the printer switched on. For example, to output the directory listing to the printer, press Ctrl-P, type

    DIR

and press Ctrl-P again.

If you forget to switch off the printer, you will realize it quickly at the next entry.

The steps just described are not suitable for printing out longer texts, since you will not be able to continue working until your printer has finished printing. A 20-page document might take half an hour to print. The DOS PRINT command therefore recognizes several options to allow better utilization of your computer.

*PRINT command*

    [d:path] PRINT [filespec,...]
       [/D:device] [/B:buffer] [/U:busytick]
       [/M:maxtick] [/S:timeslice] [/Q:queue]
       [/C] [/P] [/T]

*Syntax for PRINT*

/**D:***device* specifies the output device.

/**B:***buffer* determines the buffer size in bytes.

/**U:***busytick* defines the time that the PRINT command will wait if the printer is busy. The default setting is 1, and the time unit is 1/18 second.

/**M:***maxtick* defines how much time the PRINT command has to complete a printout, in increments of 1/18 second. The default is 2, and you can enter any value from 1 to 255.

/**S:***timeslice* defines the number of time slices. The default is 8, and you can enter any value from 1 to 255.

/**Q:***queue* specifies the maximum number of files allowed in the queue. The default is 10, and you can enter any value from 4 to 32.

**/C** deletes from the queue the specified file and all files following it on the command line.

**/P** adds the files specified in the command line to the queue.

**/T** stops the printout. The entire queue is deleted, and a message to this effect is displayed.

The printing process runs resident in the *background*. This means that you can work with an additional program in the *foreground* while printing. You should be aware, however, that you cannot readdress the printer from your program while PRINT is running.

Only the file name is found in the queue. The file is not read until it is printed.

If you modify a file that is located in the queue, PRINT will print the modified version. This means that you cannot use this command to document an old file or program status.

The first time you execute PRINT after booting the computer, you will receive a message and a prompt:

```
Name of list device [PRN]:
Resident part of PRINT installed
```

At this point, enter the device name of your printer (serial printers are usually COM1), or simply press Enter (for printers connected to a parallel port). This prompt will not appear if you state the device name directly when you access the PRINT command:

```
PRINT filename /D:PRN
```

Entering PRINT with no parameters displays the contents of the queue. If no files have been placed in the queue or if the queue no longer contains files, the following message will be displayed:

```
Print queue is empty
```
*Error*

You can specify files to be printed individually with several PRINT commands or by consecutive addresses in a single PRINT command, separated by commas. You can also specify file groups by using wildcards:
*Specification of print files*

```
PRINT   D:\WORD5\REPT???.TXT
```

All files that are to be printed can be placed into the queue at the same time, as long as the queue size specified by the /Q switch does not exceed the maximum of 32 files:
*Size of the queue*

```
PRINT filenames /Q:32
```

If the printer stops during printing (out of paper, paper jam), or if an important printout needs to be rushed through, you can remove all files from the queue with /T:
*Out of paper, paper jam*

```
PRINT /T
```

This interruption is acknowledged by a printer message.

The default values for /B, /M, /U, and /S are usually sufficient. If the printout is proceeding too slowly or if the response time of your application program in the foreground is too slow, then you will need to reset PRINT:
*Optimization*

```
PRINT /B:8192 /U:2 /M:4 /S:20
```

These values are optimal for printers with small buffers. For printers with large memory buffers (such as laser printers), set /U:1 and /M:5, and determine the optimum value for /S by experimenting. Set the buffer size of PRINT as large as possible for fast printers and printers with large memories. Remember, however, that the application program in the foreground also requires base memory.

Two commands will delete individual files or groups of files: DEL and ERASE. Both commands perform the same function.

## DEL

DEL deletes the specified files from the directory. Deleted files are still present physically, but although they can be retrieved through special utility programs (such as Norton Utilities or PC Tools Deluxe), they cannot be accessed directly with DOS commands.

*DEL*
*command*

        **DEL filespec**

Always specify the exact directory and drive when deleting a file. This will help you avoid inadvertently deleting files in the current directory:

*Syntax of*
*DEL*

        **DEL  C:\OLDDATA\*.***

If you are located in the root directory of drive C, you can also abbreviate this command as follows:

        **DEL  OLDDATA**

Specifying the name of a directory as a parameter deletes all files in that subdirectory but not the directory itself. To delete a directory, you must use the RD command.

Before deleting all files in a directory, DOS always asks whether you are sure of what you are doing:

        **Are you sure (Y/N)?**

Before you press Y, confirm that your entry will actually delete the files you want to delete.

Neither of the delete commands will delete hidden files, system files, or write-protected files. You must remove the read-only attribute with the ATTRIB command before you can delete a write-protected file, but ATTRIB cannot change the *hidden* or *system* attributes. Again, utility programs such as Q-DOS, Norton Utilities, or PC Tools Deluxe are recommended for this function (see Step 20).

## ERASE

*ERASE command*

DOS adopted the ERASE command from CP/M in order to make the conversion to DOS easier for CP/M users. Using ERASE rather than DEL has the disadvantage that the word *ERASE* requires two additional keystrokes. There is no advantage to using one over the other, since ERASE operates exactly the same as DEL does. Many DOS books advise beginners to use the ERASE command, since DEL can supposedly be easily confused with DIR. This confusion could cause the loss of important files.

*Syntax of ERASE*

```
ERASE filespec
```

DOS allows several different monitor configurations with the MODE command. You can set the desired screen mode and set the horizontal display adjustment.

## Selecting the Screen Mode

To set the desired *screen mode*, use the MODE command in the following form:

*MODE command*

    [d:path] MODE screentype

The *screentype* parameter specifies the display mode. The following are allowed: 40 (40 characters/line), 80 (80 characters/line), BW40 (monochrome, 40 characters/line), BW80 (monochrome, 80 characters/line), CO40 (color, 40 characters/line), CO80 (color, 80 characters/line) and MONO (monochrome). For example, the following command sets the screen mode for a color monitor with 80 characters per line:

    MODE CO80

## Display Adjustment

On some monitors, you must center the display. You can adjust the horizontal display either by a rotary knob on the back of the unit that adjusts the deflection, or by the MODE command if there is no such knob:

*Adjusting the display*

    [D:path] MODE [screentype],direction [,T]

To adjust, enter the MODE command with the direction option R for right or L for left. Each execution of the MODE command moves the display one column in the specified direction. You can check the adjustment by adding ,T. This option displays a test chart on the screen, which consists of

*Checking the adjustment*

eight repetitions of the sequence *0123456789* at the top of the screen and the following question at the bottom of the screen:

`Do you see the rightmost "9"? (Y/N)`

If you can see the rightmost 9, then your screen is adjusted correctly.

Communication between two computers or between a computer and a peripheral device is handled through a *serial port*. This communication operates by transferring single bits successively through a single data circuit (a channel).

The speed of this transmission is called the *baud rate*, which represents the number of bits that can be transmitted per second.

*Baud rate*

Both the transmitting device and the receiving device transfer the data at the same speed. The devices must also recognize the same control signals that are transmitted with the data for synchronization and verification. These signals are the synchronization bits, the stop bits, and the parity bit.

## Connecting a Printer

A printer is usually connected to the computer's parallel port. Unlike the serial port, this port does not need to be initialized. The parallel port is also the default port for DOS. If you want to connect an additional printer, a plotter, a modem, a mouse, or a digitizer to the serial port, you must inform DOS that the data will now be transferred through the serial port instead of through the parallel port. Use the MODE command to do this:

*Parallel port*

*Serial port*

```
MODE LPT1:=COM1
```

DOS can manage up to three parallel (LPT1 to LPT3) and four serial (COM1 to COM4) ports. Most serial cards contain two serial ports, enabling you to print one drawing on a plotter while drawing a new one with a digitizer.

## Initialization

*Adjusting the baud rate*

After you have redirected the data flow to the serial port, you will need to adapt this data flow to your printer or other connected device. Generally, this requires simply setting the transfer rate; most printers should be set at 9600 baud:

```
MODE COM1: 9600
```

Following the MODE command, specify the desired port (here COM1) and the baud rate (see below).

*Data communication*

Several additional parameters are required for setting the port for remote data communication or computer remote control:

```
MODE COM1 [:] baudrate [,parity]
     [,databits][,stopbits][,P]
```

*Parity*
*Data bits*
*Stop bits*

Options for the baud rate are 110, 150, 300, 600, 1200, 2400, 4800, 9600, and 19200 (you must have DOS 3.3 or later to use 19200 baud). You can set parity at N (none), O (odd), or E (even); the default is E. You can select either 7 or 8 data bits (default is 7) and 1 or 2 stop bits (default is 2 at a baud rate of 110; it is 1 at baud rates greater than 110). **P**, which is used with serial printers, instructs the computer to continue to attempt to send data, even if it encounters errors.

Most DOS commands report their results on the screen, since the screen is the default device for output. Input to DOS is generally intended to come through the keyboard. Input and/or output can, however, be redirected to other devices.

## Redirecting

To redirect output to the printer, enter a "greater than" character (>) along with the device name for the printer (PRN) following the desired command:

*> character*

```
DIR >PRN
```

The "greater than" character is one of three symbols used for redirecting (>, >> and <). The command in this example sends the directory listing to the printer. DIR is not the only command that can be redirected; you can redirect any DOS command that generates an output or report.

You can also record the output of a command in a file:

```
DIR >FILES.TXT
```

*Com-
mand
output in
a file*

You can use the TYPE command to examine the contents of a file:

```
TYPE FILES.TXT
```

If you repeat the command to redirect the output from the DIR command to the file FILES.TXT, the new will overwrite the old. Perhaps this is what you want to accomplish. Assume, however, that you want to list the contents of several directories, one after another, in a single file. Instead of the

*>>character*

single > character, in this case you would use a double >> character:

```
DIR >>FILES.TXT
```

With the TYPE command, you can easily check that both directories have actually been stored in this file.

*Input from a file*

So far, only output has been redirected. A command can also receive input from a file instead of from the keyboard. The following example shows the contents of the batch file FORM720.BAT:

```
FORMAT A: /N:9 /T:80 < KEYBOARD.DAT
```

*FORM720. BAT*

FORM720 formats 3.5" disks with 720Kb in a 1.44Mb drive. So that the user will not have to press any keys, the FORMAT command will receive any necessary specifications from the KEYBOARD.DAT file. This ASCII text file contains the following information:

```
<ENTER>
N<ENTER>
```

Here, *<ENTER>* means that you must press the Enter key.

## Pipes

*| symbol*

Pipes perform a different function. They direct the data flow from one program to another. The programs are written in an input string, separated by the pipe symbol (|):

```
Program 1 | Program 2 | Program 3... |
        Program n
```

Since pipes are generally used in conjunction with filters, you will find examples in the following sections on FIND, SORT, and MORE.

# Filters

Filters usually receive input data by means of redirections and pipes. This data "flows" through the filter and is changed by it in a specific manner. FIND searches for specific character strings within a file. MORE interrupts the output of a command after each screen page and waits until a key is pressed (like the /P switch of the DIR command). SORT can sort a directory listing or the contents of a file, for instance; it sorts the data it reads from standard input, then sends it to standard output.

*Filters*

# FIND

FIND is a filter that receives input from the specified or preset input device, from an input file, or from a pipe and searches it for the specified character string. The character string to be searched for is put in quotation marks in the command line:

*FIND command*

```
[d:path] FIND [/C][/N][/V] " character-
     string " [filespec...]
```

*Syntax of FIND*

Since FIND is an external DOS command, a drive and path specification can precede the command. Switches can accomplish the following:

/C counts the lines that have the *character-string* in them and displays this sum.

*Switches for FIND*

/N displays the line numbers of the lines containing the *character-string*.

/V displays all the lines that do not contain the *character string*.

*Searching individual files*

The following command shows how you could use FIND to identify all customers from Seattle listed in a customer file:

```
FIND "Seattle" CUSTOMER.DAT
```

*Output to printer*

You could redirect the result of this FIND to the printer:

```
FIND "Seattle" CUSTOMER.DAT > PRN
```

*Searching multiple files*

You can search multiple files by entering the names of the files successively in the command line, separated by blank spaces:

```
FIND    "Seattle"    CUSTOMER.DAT    HOTEL.DAT
    >   PRN
```

FIND will now display not only all customers from Seattle, but also a list of hotels you have stayed at during business trips to Seattle.

Since FIND stops searching a file as soon as it encounters a Ctrl-Z character (end-of-file marker) in it, only ASCII text files should be searched with this filter.

# MORE

*Syntax of MORE*

```
[d:path] MORE
```

*MORE command*

The MORE command is a filter that receives data and outputs it page by page. After each screen page, the display stops and the following message is displayed at the bottom of the screen:

```
- Continuation -
```

or

```
Press any key to continue...
```

The next page is displayed as soon as you press any key. MORE is often used to display long text files a page at a time:

**TYPE LONGTEXT.TXT|MORE**

You do not need to use the TYPE command if you redirect the input by using the pipe:

**MORE < LONGTEXT.TXT**

In conjunction with SORT, MORE can display a sorted directory listing or the sorted contents of a file, as you can see in the following examples.

*Long text files*

*Alternative to TYPE*

# SORT

The SORT command is a filter that receives input data and sorts it according to the specified parameters, then displays the sorted data or records it in a file:

**[d:path] SORT [/R] [/+column]**

Since SORT is an external DOS command, a drive and path specification can precede the command. Switches can accomplish the following:

*/R* sorts in descending alphabetic order.

*/+column* sorts according to the specified column.

By using a redirection or a pipe, information can be input from an input device, from a file, or from another command. The /R switch reverses the sorting order (9 to 0 and then Z to A, instead of 0 to 9 and then A to Z).

*SORT command*

*Syntax of SORT*

*Switches for SORT*

*Reversing sorting order*

*Sorting a directory*

SORT is frequently used to display the sorted contents of a directory:

```
DIR|SORT
```

*Sorting a file*

The directory itself is not sorted; only the output of the DIR command is sorted. However, just as with FIND and MORE, the SORT command can be redirected in order to rearrange data. In the following example, SORT takes data from CHAOS.DAT, sorts it by line, and records the sorted information in a file called ORDER.DAT:

```
SORT < CHAOS.DAT > ORDER.DAT
```

*Sorting by columns*

The /+*column* switch allows you to sort according to criteria found in a certain column rather than at the beginning of a line. The following command produces a directory sorted according to file name extensions:

```
DIR|SORT /+10
```

This step will introduce you to the line editor EDLIN. EDLIN does not recognize formatting commands, and you must enter or change data by line. You can quickly, but not conveniently, create or modify short ASCII files or simple batch files with this editor.

> [*d:path*] EDLIN *filespec* [/B]

*Syntax of EDLIN*

You execute EDLIN by entering the program name followed by a file name:

> EDLIN EXERCISE.TXT

*Executing EDLIN*

You can specify the optional /B switch. This will allow you to load a file that contains several Ctrl-Z (end-of-file) characters within the file instead of just one at the end. After the program is started, the EDLIN prompt appears:

*/B switch*

> *

*EDLIN prompt*

At the prompt you can enter special commands, just as you can in DOS. As a line editor, EDLIN is not user-friendly. Each line that you wish to change must be addressed individually. You cannot move from line to line with the cursor keys (as in a whole-page editor or a word processor). You have to leave the editing mode (with Ctrl-Z) to execute commands. At the EDLIN prompt, you can then enter commands consisting of a letter and options.

All EDLIN commands are thoroughly discussed here in alphabetical order. Keep in mind that the commands from APPEND to WRITE must be entered at the EDLIN prompt, not at the DOS prompt. It is especially important not to confuse the APPEND command of EDLIN with the APPEND command that you can enter at the DOS prompt.

# A (APPEND)

*Loading additional lines*

The APPEND command of EDLIN loads additional lines of the file from the floppy disk or hard disk into RAM memory. This is only necessary with files that are too large to fit into 75 percent of the free RAM memory.

Assuming that enough memory is available (refer to the W or WRITE command below), you can, for example, load 15 text lines from a file with this command:

```
15A
```

If the maximum that can be loaded from the floppy or hard disk is 15 lines or less, you will receive this message:

*Error*

```
End of input file
```

# C (COPY)

*Copying lines*

The COPY command of EDLIN allows you to make one or more copies of lines of text. This can be useful in writing a batch file if it contains several program segments (commands or groups of commands) that are similar.

The following command copies lines 2 to 4 six times and inserts them ahead of line 20:

```
2,4,20,6C
```

Line 20 then becomes line 38. Six copies of lines 2 through 4 now make up lines 20 to 37.

# D (DELETE)

*Deleting lines*

The DELETE command of EDLIN erases lines from your file. Deleting lines changes the line numbers of the lines within the file, since the deleted lines are replaced by the following lines. The total number of lines is thus reduced by the number of lines deleted.

You can delete one line or several successive lines with this command. A line is deleted when you specify the appropriate line number:

```
21D
```

In this case, line 21 is deleted. If the file contained 24 lines before deleting, it is now only 23 lines long. What was previously line 22 now becomes 21, 23 becomes 22, and 24 becomes 23. You can delete lines 21 to 23 with one command:

```
21,23D
```

## Line Number (LINE EDIT)

The LINE EDIT command consists only of the line number of the desired line. You can change any line of a file that is currently stored in the memory.

*Editing individual lines*

Entering 19, for example, displays line 19 followed by an empty line on which corrections can be made:

```
*19
        19:*This line is being eded.
        19:*This line is being edited.
```

As at the DOS prompt, function keys are available in EDLIN so that you will not need to reenter every character. Table 13.1 contains a list of the available function keys. You could correct the example line quickly by pressing F3 and then moving the cursor with the ← key until it is at the first *d* of *eded*. You could also get to the same spot by pressing F4 and *d*. Next, press the Ins key to switch on the insert mode, and enter the missing letters *i* and *t*. The F3 key displays the rest of the line, and you can complete the correction by pressing Enter.

*Function keys*

| Function Key | Action |
|---|---|
| F1 | Displays one character of the line being edited. |
| F2*character* | Displays all characters of the line being edited, from the beginning of the line up to *character*. |
| F3 | Displays all characters from the current cursor position to the end of the line. |
| F4*character* | Skips over all characters of the line being edited, from the beginning of the line up to the specified *character*. |

*Table 13.1: Function keys of EDLIN*

## E (END)

*Exiting from EDLIN and saving*

The END command terminates EDLIN. Any changes to the edited file are saved, and the file is closed.

For security, EDLIN creates a copy of the prior version of the file on the floppy or hard disk as a .BAK file. To save your changes, simply enter the following command:

```
E
```

## I (INSERT)

*Inserting lines*

Programming batch files or writing a short text frequently

requires the insertion of lines in an existing text file. Entering the command

        *14I

results in:

        14:*

Each line that you now write (until you terminate the EDLIN mode with Ctrl-C) will be inserted in your file, beginning with line 14. All following lines will be correspondingly displaced.

## L (LIST)

The LIST command of EDLIN displays a portion of the edited file on the screen. Entering the LIST command with no options displays the first line of the edited file:

        L

*Displaying lines*

With relatively long files, you can choose to display a specific section. The following command, for example, displays lines 19 to 32:

        19,32L

## M (MOVE)

The MOVE command of EDLIN removes a block of lines from one location in your file and inserts it at another location within the file.

*Moving blocks of lines*

The following example illustrates how to insert a line block—lines 4 through 14—in front of line 19:

        4,14,19M

# P (PAGE)

*Paging
through
the file*

The PAGE command of EDLIN permits you to browse through an entire file or through a chosen section. The following command displays lines 5 through 65:

        5,65P

In contrast to the LIST command, PAGE defines the last displayed line as the new current line. Entering the PAGE command without options will display the entire file by pages.

# Q (QUIT)

*Ending
EDLIN*

You normally use the QUIT command if an incorrect file name has been specified when executing EDLIN.

You can use QUIT to leave EDLIN without saving any changes that you have made unintentionally or as an exercise. To leave EDLIN this way, enter

        Q

*Safety
prompt*

For safety's sake, you are then asked whether you actually wish to disregard all changes:

        **Abort edit (Y/N)?**

Entering N returns you to EDLIN. Entering Y takes you to the DOS prompt without saving the changes of the last EDLIN session.

# R (REPLACE)

The REPLACE command of EDLIN can quickly eliminate repeated errors. You can also use it to speed up the input of text. To do this, enter abbreviations for words that occur frequently. Then use REPLACE to replace the abbreviations with the desired text.

The following REPLACE command replaces the character string *dlag* with the character string *Dear Ladies and Gentlemen* (press Ctrl-Z to display the ^Z character):

*Replacing character strings*

```
1Rdlag^ZDear Ladies and Gentlemen
```

The next example shows how dangerous the REPLACE command can be if it is used incorrectly. This shows REPLACE replacing the letter *i* with *a* throughout the entire text:

```
1Ri^Za
```

This replacement is not reversible. If you make this kind of error, it is best to leave EDLIN with Q.

To confirm each replacement, use the question mark (**?**):

*Confirming replacements*

```
1?Ri^Za
```

The program will stop after each *i* to ask if you want to replace it with an *a*.

## S (SEARCH)

The SEARCH command of EDLIN locates lines that contain the sought-for character string. You can search the entire file, or you can specify a particular range of lines to be searched.

*Searching for character strings*

You can search for all lines in a batch file that contain the FOR command by specifying line 1 as the beginning line and accepting the end of the file as the default specification for the ending line. Including a question mark (?) causes the SEARCH command to stop after it finds each occurrence of the character string to ask if you are interested in this particular line:

```
1?SFOR
```

If the question mark is not inserted, the entire file will be searched and all lines containing the specified character string will be displayed.

## T (TRANSFER)

*Joining two files*

The TRANSFER command of EDLIN permits you to join two files. To do this, it loads a specified file to the desired location within the file being edited. The incoming file is inserted before the line specified in the command.

Using this command, you could, for example, insert the batch file HEADING.BAT (see Step 14) at the beginning of another batch file for documentation:

```
1T HEADING.BAT
```

## W (WRITE)

*Writing files*

EDLIN will not load a large file completely into memory if it would occupy more than 75 percent of the available memory space. In this case, you would only be able to edit the loaded portion of the file and then write the modified lines to the disk or hard disk with WRITE, thus freeing up memory space for additional lines from the file (see the A or APPEND command of EDLIN).

Assuming you had already edited the first 40 lines of the loaded file and wanted to write these files to your hard disk, you would enter the following command:

```
40W
```

## Step 14

# Batch Files

Batch files are compilations of selected DOS commands, program names, and special batch file commands that can only be used in batch files. Because they use these commands, batch files can become complex and powerful programs that include variables, conditional jumps, loops, and subprograms.

## Creating Batch Files

You can create small batch files with the COPY CON: command, although it might be more convenient to use the ED-LIN line editor or your word processor for this. A batch file must always be an ASCII text file. You must observe several rules when you create batch files:

1. Don't use the name of a DOS command or another EXE or COM program as a batch file name, since this can sometimes cause the wrong file to be executed.

2. The batch file name can have no more than eight characters and cannot contain the following punctuation marks or special characters: . " / \ [ ] : | < > + = ; ,
   It must always have a .BAT extension.

3. Batch files will not recognize preset drive and path statements for executing external DOS commands or other programs, even though these paths might be recognized at a DOS prompt. The program files must therefore be found in the current directory or be accessible through a path (PATH command).

4. If the AUTOEXEC.BAT batch file is stored in the root directory, DOS will automatically execute it when the program is booted.

## Entering Comments with REM

A batch file should always contain comments, so that any user can quickly understand the intended function of each file and of the commands or command groups that the file executes.

*REM command*

Random comments that are not to be displayed can be inserted with the REM command if ECHO is set OFF. You can read these comments, however, when the file is displayed with the TYPE command, through EDLIN, or within a word processor.

*Syntax of REM*

```
REM [comment]
```

Any *comment* following a REM command can contain up to 123 characters. The DOS symbols for redirection (<, >, >>), pipes (|), and so on must be set in quotation marks (" "). You can use DOS commands in the comment, and these do not need to be placed in quotation marks. The following example shows how you can document a file's purpose, function, and current status at the beginning of a large batch file:

```
@ECHO OFF          •
REM name..............: file name
REM purpose...........: task of batch file
REM programmer........: your name
REM last update.......: mm-dd-yy
REM input parameters..: parameters, sepa-
                        rated by commas
REM %1 = abbreviation.: data type of
                        the parameter
REM %n = abbreviation.: data type of
                        the parameter
```

This program segment needs to be set up only once. The file

with this comment entry can then be copied and used for all batch files.

## Displaying Messages

*Syntax of ECHO*

```
ECHO [ON|OFF|character-string]
```

The commands executed by a batch file are normally displayed on the screen. You can turn off this screen display with the ECHO command:

*ECHO command*

```
ECHO OFF
```

The results of the commands are still displayed on the screen, but the screen protocol is turned off until you enter

```
ECHO ON
```

ECHO can also send a line of text to the printer or write it to a file:

```
ECHO Print this sentence now! >LPT1
```

You can also display messages to the user on the screen:

```
ECHO This is an important screen message!
```

After starting this batch file, the user would see the following lines on the screen:

```
This is an important screen message!
```

Entering the ECHO command without parameters displays the current ECHO status:

```
ECHO
ECHO is on
```

## Interrupting a Batch File

The PAUSE command is used to interrupt a batch file so that the user can review the displayed data at leisure.

```
PAUSE [character-string]
```

You can use the optional *character-string* to tell the user what to do at the pause. The user can also abort the processing of the batch file by pressing Ctrl-C and answering Y to the following question:

```
Terminate batch job (Y/N)?
```

If ECHO is switched on (ECHO ON), the word *PAUSE* and the specified *character-string*, if any, are displayed before the message

```
Strike a key when ready . . .
```

The message can also be turned off by the following commands:

```
@ECHO OFF
ECHO character-string
PAUSE
```

The @ character turns off the display of the ECHO OFF command, and the command ECHO OFF turns off the display of the following commands. The following example shows how you can tell the user that the batch file can be aborted:

```
PAUSE  Press <Ctrl><C> to return to
operating system or
```

The following lines will then appear on the screen:

```
Press <Ctrl><C> to return to operating
system or
Strike a key when ready . . .
```

# Executing a Batch File and Variable Parameters

A batch file is executed the same way a DOS command is: by entering the name followed by any necessary parameters. The parameters are stored in the program as variable parameters. The variables %0 to %9 can be used for this. With the SHIFT command, you can use more than ten variables in a batch program by allocating the ten available variables sequentially several times.

*Variable parameters %0 to %9*

*SHIFT command*

```
SHIFT
```

*Syntax of SHIFT*

Here's a simple example: if you enter

```
BATCH1 yes no maybe <Enter>
```

then

```
%1=yes
%2=no
%3=maybe
```

and after the SHIFT command is issued,

```
%1=no
%2=maybe
```

Now let's look at another example. When executing a batch file with 20 parameters, for instance, variable %0 contains the file name. The first input parameter is stored in variable %1, the second in %2, and so on, until the ninth parameter is stored in %9. The first time the SHIFT command is executed, the value that was previously assigned to variable %2 is shifted to variable %1. The value now assigned to variable %2 was previously the value of variable %3, and so on. At the now unassigned variable %9, you can access a tenth input parameter that you could previously not access.

This system has one disadvantage: the first input parameter (originally stored in %1) can no longer be accessed. The repeated use of the SHIFT command allows sequential access to all 20 parameters of the example, but only nine can be directly accessed at any given time. Any values lying before the first accessible parameter are unavailable for this run of the batch file.

## Loops with FOR

*FOR*
*command*

The FOR command forms a loop through which a command is run several times with different parameters. This is roughly equivalent to loops in high-level programming languages such as BASIC, Pascal, or C. The FOR command is not as powerful as its corresponding element in the programming languages.

*Syntax of*
*FOR*

        FOR %%variable IN (values) DO commands

You can let DOS commands, subcommands in batch files, or batch files run repeatedly. For example, assume that your computer has five drives, A to E. With a single line in the batch file, you can execute the CHKDSK command five times, checking each drive in turn:

        FOR %%D IN (A B C D E) DO CHKDSK %%D

You must be careful that the variable name you specify (here, %%D) is not a word reserved for use by DOS.

## Unconditional Branching

*GOTO*
*command*

It is often necessary to skip several commands in processing a batch file and continue the program from another point (branching). Likewise, certain segments of programs can be accessed and repeated (looping). You can execute such program jumps with the GOTO command. You will find the following line, for example, in many batch files:

```
GOTO END
```

or, with a colon,

```
GOTO :END
```

Executing this command at any point in the batch file causes the program to skip to the line marked with the label :END. This is referred to as an unconditional jump—that is, a jump to another point in the file that is not subject to any conditions.

```
GOTO [:]label
```

*Syntax of GOTO*

## Conditional Branching

In conditional branching, a command is executed only if a specified condition is true or false. You can use the skip command GOTO this way. Thus you can make jumps within the batch file dependent on a condition.

Conditions are queried with the IF command. For example,

*IF command*

```
IF A==B THEN GOTO :START
```

means simply "If A is equal to B, then continue execution of the program from the START label. If A is not equal to B, continue execution of the command from the next line."

The IF command can perform various comparisons and execute specified commands depending on the results of those comparisons (true or false).

```
IF [NOT] condition command
```

*Syntax of IF*

A *condition* is evaluated as true or false, determining the further course of the program. The following operands and operators are allowed:

*Operators for condition*

- ERRORLEVEL *code* is evaluated as true if the return code of the most recently exited program is greater than or equal to *code*, where *code* is a whole number.

- *character-string1* == *character-string2* checks for agreement between character strings, distinguishing between uppercase and lowercase letters. If both character strings are identical, the condition is true.

- EXIST *filespec* checks whether a file with the specified file specification is located in the specified directory.

The *command* (normally a DOS command) is executed if the *condition* is fulfilled—that is, if the *condition* is evaluated as true.

NOT inverts the result of the query condition. Thus, if *condition* is false, then NOT *condition* is true.

The following example illustrates a conditional branching. The file is processed as far as the :Error label, as long as no parameter was specified when the batch file was executed; otherwise, the program skips directly to the :End label.

```
ECHO OFF
IF %1~==~GOTO :Error
GOTO :End
:Error
ECHO No parameter was specified!
:End
ECHO At the end!
```

The comparison operator EXIST is often used with installation programs or data backup programs to check whether the correct disk has been inserted, as in the following program excerpt:

```
:TEST1
IF EXIST A:DISK1.DAT GOTO :DISK1
GOTO :ERROR1
:DISK1
COPY A:*.*
GOTO :TEST2
:ERROR1
CLS
ECHO Incorrect disk has been inserted.
ECHO Please insert disk 1!
GOTO :TEST1
```

In this example, if the file DISK1.DAT is located on the disk in drive A, the program is continued from the :DISK1 label. The command following this label copies all files from drive A into the current directory. Program processing then continues from the TEST2 label (not shown in this example).

If a specified file name is not found, the instruction GOTO :DISK1 is ignored. The next command jumps to :ERROR1 instead. The user is given an opportunity to insert the correct disk. This roughly corresponds to an IF...THEN...ELSE construction in a higher-level programming language.

*IF...*
*THEN...*
*ELSE*
*construction*

## Subprograms

The CALL command permits the execution of subprograms. With this command, a second batch file can be executed from within another batch file. After the program has processed this second batch file, control returns to the original file, and the next command in that first file is executed.

*CALL*
*command*

**CALL** *filespec*

*Syntax of*
*CALL*

*Recursive calls*

*Continuous loops*

Recursive calls are possible within batch files. This means that a batch file can execute itself an infinite number of times. You must make certain that the program is ended and does not create a continuous loop.

A simple batch file named LETTER.BAT illustrates the execution of a second batch file with CALL:

```
CALL HEADING
CALL ADDRESS %1
CALL TEXT %2
CALL CLOSING
```

The batch file HEADING.BAT prints several lines with the name of your company, the date, and your name. ADDRESS.BAT prints an address using the address file reported in variable parameter %1. TEXT.BAT prints the text file specified in variable parameter %2, and the letter is completed with CLOSING.BAT.

As you experiment with these commands and create your own batch files to streamline your work, you can save a lot of time entering commands.

The files CONFIG.SYS AND AUTOEXEC.BAT configure DOS. If your DOS system is already installed, you might never need to change these files. Changes are almost always necessary, however, if you install a new application program or expand your system with peripheral devices such as a mouse.

## CONFIG.SYS

The CONFIG.SYS file contains a special type of DOS command: the configuration commands, which load device drivers and change default DOS parameters. These commands cannot be entered at the DOS prompt or used in a batch file such as AUTOEXEC.BAT. This batch file can contain anything you can enter at the DOS prompt.

*Configuration commands*

When the system is booted, the CONFIG.SYS file is read and DOS is customized corresponding to the settings recorded in this file. This means that any change to the file will not be read until the next time the system is started. Switch the computer off and then back on, or press the key combination Ctrl-Alt-Del to have your changes become effective.

## BREAK

BREAK is a configuration command that also functions as an internal command. BREAK makes it easier to interrupt programs: when BREAK is switched on (with ON), DOS looks to the keyboard more frequently to see if the key combination Ctrl-C or Ctrl-Break has been entered.

*BREAK command*

        BREAK=[ON|OFF]

*Syntax of BREAK*

High-level programming languages and some application programs use Ctrl-Break during programming in order to interrupt programs that are in a continuous loop. As a typical DOS user, you can use this program-interrupt feature to interrupt batch files or stop DOS commands.

## BUFFERS

*BUFFERS command*

Each time a floppy disk or hard disk is accessed, a buffer is required. You should set the BUFFERS value as Table 15.1 suggests, or according to the recommendations in the manuals for your application software. Enter the BUFFERS value in your CONFIG.SYS file with the following line:

```
BUFFERS=20
```

*Memory allocation*

DOS will now reserve 10,240 bytes (20 × 512 bytes) for a temporary input/output buffer. Entering

```
BUFFERS=10
```

saves some memory space (5120 bytes), but you might find that setting BUFFERS to 10 will be insufficient for programs that keep a lot of files open.

*Values for BUFFERS*

| BUFFERS Value | RAM (Kb) |
|---|---|
| 15 | 512 |
| 20 | 640 (XT) |
| 40 | 640 (AT) |

*Table 15.1: Recommended values for BUFFERS*

## COUNTRY

*COUNTRY command*

DOS is used in many nations; there are different formats for writing the time and date in many of these countries. You can use the COUNTRY command to select one of the 21 country codes, as well as to set a desired ASCII character set table (code page) and currency formatting. The COUNTRY setting controls the date format of the DATE and TIME commands and of other commands that require output or processing of the date.

The following command allows use of the formats used in Israel (country code 972) in conjunction with international code page 850:

```
COUNTRY=972,850,C:\DOS\COUNTRY.SYS
```

The system file COUNTRY.SYS locates COUNTRY in the subdirectory DOS on drive C. To find the correct values, consult Table 15.2, which lists the available country codes.

| *Country* | *Country Code* |
|-----------|----------------|
| Arabia | 785 |
| Australia | 061 |
| Belgium | 032 |
| Canada (English) | 001 |
| Canada (French) | 002 |
| Denmark | 045 |
| Germany | 049 |
| Finland | 358 |
| France | 033 |
| Israel (Hebraic) | 972 |
| Italy | 039 |
| Latin America | 003 |
| Netherlands | 031 |

*Table 15.2: The international country codes of DOS*

| Country | Country Code |
|---|---|
| Norway | 047 |
| Portugal | 351 |
| Spain | 034 |
| Sweden | 046 |
| Switzerland | 041 |
| United Kingdom | 044 |
| United States | 001 |

*Table 15.2: The international country codes of DOS (cont.)*

## DEVICE

*DEVICE command*

DEVICE loads a device driver into the standard memory. You can put this command in the CONFIG.SYS file as often as necessary. Some drivers must be loaded in an exact sequence; also consider that each driver occupies memory space. The following command line customizes the driver for an attached monitor to accommodate an EGA screen and the code page 437:

```
DEVICE=C:\DISPLAY.SYS CON:=(EGA,437,2)
```

In Step 16, you will become familiar with device drivers that you can access through MS/PC-DOS 3.3 using the DEVICE command. Note that hardware manufacturers sometimes provide device drivers for their products.

## FCBS

*File control blocks*

*Memory requirement*

In older DOS versions—particularly in Version 1.x—files were accessed by means of file control blocks (FCBs). These are segments in the standard memory, approximately 40 bytes in size, that hold file names and other file attributes open for

DOS. Without specification of the FCBs, DOS creates four segments. If your application program operates with file control blocks and opens more files, you must specify the FCBS command in the CONFIG.SYS file. For example,

*FCBS command*

```
FCBS=10,6
```

instructs DOS to open a maximum of ten files with FCBs. Six of these files can remain open. If a program tries to open 13 files, DOS holds the first six files open. Then three of the first four opened files are closed, so that the eleventh, twelfth, and thirteenth files can be opened.

## FILES

The FILES command specifies the number of files that can be opened simultaneously. Consult the manuals of your application programs to determine the maximum number of files that will be opened, and set the FILES command correspondingly. The command line

*FILES command*

```
FILES=25
```

allows your application program to hold up to 25 files open simultaneously. More recent database and network programs usually require even larger values. You should also consider that an input/output buffer with a size of 48 bytes is created for each additional file. A FILES command with the maximum number of 255 buffers requires more than 11Kb of memory space.

## LASTDRIVE

LASTDRIVE expands the default setting from five drive identifiers up to 26 (A–Z). You will need this command if the total number of physical drives, logical drives in an expanded

*LAST-DRIVE command*

partition, the RAM disk, and the simulated drives created with SUBST is greater than five. Entering

```
LASTDRIVE=J
```

allows you to use five additional letters (F, G, H, I, and J) as drive designators.

# SHELL

*SHELL command*

When DOS is booted, the SHELL command allows the user to change the program used for a command interpreter. The program used must be designed for the purpose. This allows system programmers to use their own command interpreter in place of COMMAND.COM. You can also use the SHELL command in conjunction with the /E switch:

*/E switch*

```
SHELL=SUPER.COM /E:500 /P
```

*/P switch*

With this command, you can permanently load the specially developed command interpreter SUPER.COM to a system environment of 500 bytes. The /P switch forces the command interpreter to remain resident in the standard memory and to execute the AUTOEXEC.BAT file if one is present. Note that /E and /P are parameters for COMMAND.COM, and other command interpreters will not always support them.

# STACKS

*STACKS command*

The STACKS command prevents the system from locking if it encounters multiple hardware interrupts. It allocates memory for stacking these hardware interrupts; this memory is therefore called stack memory. When a hardware interrupt occurs, it is allocated to the first stack area. The next interrupt is stacked "above," and so on. When several hardware interrupts occur successively, the most recent interrupt is retrieved first from the stack. If the stack is completely filled, the system will lock in spite of the command.

*Syntax of*
*STACKS*

> **STACKS=***number***,***size*

The *number* parameter specifies the number of stacks (8 to 64), and the *size* parameter specifies the size of each stack area (32 to 512). You can use

> **STACKS=0,0**

when you don't want any memory allocated for stacks.

## AUTOEXEC.BAT

*AUTO-
EXEC.BAT*

You can enter any DOS command and any special batch file commands in the AUTOEXEC.BAT file. The file is read when the system is booted, and the commands found there are executed. Generally, the file contains at least the commands DATE, TIME, and VER (see Step 3); however, machines with a built-in clock (AT, 386, 486, and some XT models) do not need DATE and TIME. You can also use the commands APPEND, PATH, PROMPT, SET, and SHARE to customize your system. These commands are discussed below.

## APPEND

*APPEND
command*

When the APPEND command is executed, it is loaded resident in the memory, thus occupying memory space. APPEND tells DOS where to look for data files—any files that are not .EXE, .COM, or .BAT files. Data files include application documents and overlay files (.OVL, .DAT, .DBF, .NDX). For example, the command

> **APPEND C:\DOS;C:\WORD;C:\DBASE**

searches for data files in the three specified directories on drive C.

The first time APPEND is loaded, you can use the format

*Syntax of APPEND*

    `[d:path] APPEND [d1:path1][;d2:path2...]`

or

    `[d:path] APPEND [/X][/E]`

After APPEND has been loaded, use

    `APPEND d1:path1[;d2:path2...]`

or

    `APPEND[;]`

*Switches for APPEND*

**/X** switches on the processing of search methods *Search First, Find First*, and *Exec Functions*.

**/E** stores the path in the DOS environment.

**;** erases all assignments.

## PATH

*PATH command*

PATH searches the specified directories for programs (.EXE, .COM, and .BAT). The directories are searched in the sequence in which they are listed in the PATH command. If two programs with the same name are stored in directories in the path, the program located in the directory that was specified first is executed. For example, the command

    `PATH F:\;C:\;C:\DOS;C:\WORD;C:\DBASE;`
    `C:\123`

searches the root directory on drive F and the five specified directories on drive C for .EXE, .COM, and .BAT files.

You can use

```
PATH [d1:path1][;d2:path2...]
```

or

```
PATH[;]
```

where the semicolon (;) cancels the path assignments.

## PROMPT

PROMPT changes the DOS prompt. If the ANSI.SYS device driver is activated, it also has two additional uses, which will be discussed in Steps 17 and 18.

```
PROMPT [character-string|parameter]
```

The appearance of the prompt is established by a character string that always begins with a dollar sign ($) followed by another character. You can arrange several of these character strings in a series to produce a prompt with as much information as needed.

Here is an example of a handy DOS prompt:

```
PROMPT $D$B$T$H$H$H$H$H$H$B$P$G
```

This displays the following prompt:

```
Thur 1-18-1990|7:33p|C:\PCTOOLS>
```

Pressing Enter then displays the current time:

```
Thur 1-18-1990|7:34p|C:\PCTOOLS>
```

| | Character Combination | Description |
|---|---|---|
| *Metasymbols for PROMPT* | $$ | $ sign |
| | $t | Time |
| | $d | Date |
| | $p | Current directory of default drive |
| | $v | DOS version number |
| | $n | Current drive |
| | $g | > character |
| | $l | < character |
| | $b | I character |
| | $q | = character |
| | $h | Backspace function |
| | $e | Esc character |
| | $_ | Carriage return and line feed |

*Table 15.3: Parameters for setting PROMPT (metasymbols)*

## SET

*SET command*

SET changes character strings into environment variables that are stored in the DOS environment. This DOS environment is a special memory area for system settings that the user can use with SET.

*Syntax of SET*

```
SET [name=[parameter]]
```

*DOS environment*

Entering SET without parameters displays the current contents of the DOS environment:

```
COMSPEC=C:\COMMAND.COM
PATH=C:\DOS;C:;D:\WORD5
```

The SET command can now change the setting of the PATH command without actually using the PATH command:

```
SET PATH=C:\;C:\DOS;C:\PCTOOLS;D:\WORD5;
    D:\WIN386
```

## SHARE

The SHARE command makes it possible to share files in a network situation (file sharing). It is loaded resident in the memory after execution and can only be removed from the memory by certain DOS utilities or by rebooting the system.

```
SHARE [/F:filespec][/L:locks]
```

*Syntax of SHARE*

/F establishes how much information the SHARE command can manage through opened files. Each opened file requires space for the file names and additional information; the default is 2048 bytes (2Kb). /L establishes the maximum number of locks; the default is 20 system locks.

*/F switch*

*/L switch*

## Virtual Drives

You will need the ASSIGN command to work with programs to access a drive that is not present in your system. The AS-SIGN command redirects inquiries for this drive to a drive that actually exists. JOIN and SUBST operate differently. JOIN connects two drives to a virtual directory. SUBST does the opposite and converts a directory on your hard disk into a virtual drive. All three commands can be placed in the AUTOEXEC.BAT file if they are used frequently. Usually, they are entered as needed from the DOS prompt.

# ASSIGN

ASSIGN directs all inquiries for a certain drive to another drive. These reassignments take place with the help of parameters. Entering the ASSIGN command without parameters cancels all current assignments.

The following example shows how the ASSIGN command is used with an older program that, even though it is installed on the hard disk, always accesses drive A:

        **ASSIGN A=C**

ASSIGN should never be used in conjunction with the commands BACKUP, JOIN, LABEL, PRINT, RESTORE, or SUBST. The reassignments performed with ASSIGN are ignored by the DISKCOMP, DISKCOPY, and FORMAT commands. Some application programs access drives directly through BIOS calls. Such calls cannot be redirected with ASSIGN.

        **[*d:path*] ASSIGN [*sourcedrive=
            targetdrive*][...]**

# JOIN

JOIN treats a drive as if it were a subdirectory of another drive. This does not work if the drive has been created with SUBST and is therefore not physically present. The JOIN command has three command formats. The first format displays all drives and directories that have been connected by the JOIN command; the second executes the connection; and the third releases the connection:

        **[*d:path*] JOIN**
        **[*d:path*] JOIN *sourcedrive*
            *targetdrive:path***
        **[*d:path*] JOIN *sourcedrive* [/D]**

The **/D** switch cancels all assignments of JOIN.

There are two main applications of JOIN. The first redirects the output of a program from a directory on a hard disk to a floppy disk:

```
JOIN A: C:\WIN386\CORELDRW
```

This is useful when drawings are being created and are being archived on floppy disks in order to save space on the hard drive.

The second application is generally used with older programs that were written for operation on floppy-disk drives. Here, you can use JOIN in place of the ASSIGN command, and you can redirect the the outputs and inputs from the floppy-disk drive to a directory on C:

```
JOIN C: A:\
```

# SUBST

The SUBST command creates a virtual disk drive from a directory. All subdirectories that have been replaced by virtual drives can be displayed. You can also delete the virtual drive with SUBST. The following command creates a drive G:

*SUBST command*

```
SUBST G: C:\WORD\TEXT\SCHOOL
```

The SUBST command can also fool older programs that search for program files in drive A and data files in drive B. If you create the directories C:\OLDPROG for the program and C:\OLDPROG\DATA for the data files:

```
SUBST A: C:\OLDPROG
SUBST B: C:\OLDPROG\DATA
```

The syntax formats for SUBST are as follows:

```
[d:path] SUBST
[d:path] SUBST newdrive path
[d:path] SUBST newdrive /D
```

The /D switch cancels all assignments of SUBST.

# Step 16

# Device Drivers

DOS automatically loads standard drivers for input/output devices such as monitors, printers, disk drives, and hard disk when the system is booted. In Step 15, you were introduced to the DEVICE command with which other drivers can be loaded and individually installed. This step will introduce the drivers that are supplied with DOS.

If you purchase a mouse, a digitizer, or any other device to add to your system, you will usually receive a special driver for that device with your purchase. If you do, refer to the documentation for your device to obtain installation instructions.

*Special drivers*

## ANSI.SYS

ANSI.SYS includes functions for cursor control, for adjusting screen display (colors and mode), and for keyboard mapping (see Step 17). Some application programs utilize these options and thus require this driver.

Other programs, on the other hand, will not operate correctly when ANSI.SYS has been loaded. Always check your software documentation to see if ANSI.SYS is necessary.

You can use ANSI.SYS functions with DOS commands as well. One example of this is the keyboard reassignment explained in Step 17. You can apply the techniques used to reassign a keyboard to adjusting the screen display and cursor. Tables 16.1 to 16.3 list the ANSI escape sequences required for this.

*Adjusting screen display*

Before you can use ANSI.SYS, you must install the device drivers using the DEVICE command in the CONFIG.SYS file:

```
DEVICE=[d:path]ANSI.SYS
```

After your system installs ANSI.SYS, you can enter an ANSI control code following the PROMPT command, or you can use the code in batch files. The tables contain the ANSI codes that you can use with the PROMPT command.

*Screen attributes*

| Action | ANSI Code | MDA | CGA | EGA | VGA |
|---|---|---|---|---|---|
| switch off attribute | $e[0m | Y | Y | Y | Y |
| bold print | $e[1m | Y | Y | Y | Y |
| underscore | $e[4m | Y | N | N | N |
| blink | $e[5m | Y | N | N | N |
| reverse display | $e[7m | Y | Y | Y | Y |
| invisible text | $e[8m | Y | N | N | N |
| black foreground | $e[30m | N | Y | Y | Y |
| red foreground | $e[31m | N | Y | Y | Y |
| green foreground | $e[32m | N | Y | Y | Y |
| yellow foreground | $e[33m | N | Y | Y | Y |
| blue foreground | $e[34m | N | Y | Y | Y |
| magenta foreground | $e[35m | N | Y | Y | Y |
| cyan foreground | $e[36m | N | Y | Y | Y |
| white foreground | $e[37m | N | Y | Y | Y |
| black background | $e[40m | N | Y | Y | Y |
| red background | $e[41m | N | Y | Y | Y |
| green background | $e[42m | N | Y | Y | Y |

*Table 16.1: Screen attributes*

| | | | | | |
|---|---|---|---|---|---|
| yellow background | $e[43m | N | Y | Y | Y |
| blue background | $e[44m | N | Y | Y | Y |
| magenta background | $e[45m | N | Y | Y | Y |
| cyan background | $e[46m | N | Y | Y | Y |
| white background | $e[47m | N | Y | Y | Y |

*Table 16.1: Screen attributes (cont.)*

| *Activating Screen Mode* | *ANSI Code* | *Screen mode on* |
|---|---|---|
| 40 characters × 25 lines monochrome, text mode | $e[=0h | |
| 40 characters × 25 lines color, text mode | $e[=1h | |
| 80 characters × 25 lines monochrome, text mode | $e[=2h | |
| 80 characters × 25 lines color, text mode | $e[=3h | |
| 320×200 pixels 4-color, graphics mode | $e[=4h | |
| 320×200 pixels 4-color, color burst disabled, graphics mode | $e[=5h | |
| 640×200 pixels monochrome, graphics mode | $e[=6h | |

| *Switching Screen Mode Off* | *ANSI Code* | *Screen mode off* |
|---|---|---|
| 40 characters × 25 lines monochrome, text mode | $e[=0h | |
| 40 characters × 25 lines color, text mode | $e[=1h | |
| 80 characters × 25 lines monochrome, text mode | $e[=2h | |
| 80 characters × 25 lines color, text mode | $e[=3h | |
| 320×200 pixels color, graphics mode | $e[=4h | |
| 320×200 pixels 4-color, color burst disabled, graphics mode | $e[=5h | |
| 640×200 pixels 2-color, graphics mode | $e[=6h | |

*Table 16.2: Screen mode*

*Screen control*

| Action | ANSI Code |
|---|---|
| Moves cursor to specified position. | $e[*line*;*column*H |
| Moves cursor to specified position. | $e[*line*;*column*f |
| Moves cursor *number* of lines up. | $e[*number*A |
| Moves cursor *number* of lines down. | $e[*number*B |
| Moves cursor right the specified *number* of columns. | $e[*number*C |
| Moves cursor left the specified *number* of columns. | $e[*number*D |
| Gives a report of current cursor position (used with $e[6n). | $e[*line*;*column*R |
| Console driver reports an escape sequence at cursor position. | $e[6n |
| Stores cursor position. | $e[s |
| Moves cursor to stored position. | $e[u |
| Erases the screen. | $e[2J |
| Erases from cursor to end of line. | $e[K |

*Table 16.3: Screen control*

## DISPLAY.SYS

*Displaying foreign languages*

The DISPLAY.SYS driver enables you to display foriegn languages. To display characters on the screen, DISPLAY.SYS must have access to information files such as EGA.CPI and LCD.CPI.

Like all drivers, DISPLAY.SYS must be loaded with the DEVICE command:

```
DISPLAY.SYS CON[:]=( screentype
      [,[codepage][,n][(n,m)]])
```

For *screentype* you can enter MONO, CGA, EGA, or LCD. There is no data file for VGA cards; instead of VGA, identify EGA as the screen type. The *codepage* parameter represents the character set table of the monitor. The command will recognize the codes 437, 850, 860, 863, and 865. Use the parameter *n* to inform DOS how many code pages will be available for swapping in and out; you can enter a value between 0 and 12. The *m* parameter sets the number of secondary character fonts that are supported by each code page. Its value depends on the display adapter: 0 for monochrome or CGA, or 1 to 12 for EGA or LCD.

*Screen types*

*Code pages*

*Secondary fonts*

This is an example of a DISPLAY.SYS call:

```
DEVICE=C:\DOS\DISPLAY.SYS CON=(EGA,437,2)
```

If you use DISPLAY.SYS and ANSI.SYS together in the CONFIG.SYS file, the DEVICE command for ANSI.SYS must be placed before the command for DISPLAY.SYS.

## DRIVER.SYS

DRIVER.SYS can assign one or more logical drive identifiers to a physical drive. You can define the properties of the logical drive with DRIVER.SYS. The driver has the following syntax:

*Defining logical drives*

```
DEVICE=DRIVER.SYS/D: nnn[/T:ttt] [/S:ss]
     [/H:hh] [/C] [/N] [/F:f]
```

The options have the following meanings:

**D:***nnn* is the drive number of the available physical drive (0 to 127 for floppy disks, 128 to 255 for hard disks).

/T:*ttt* specifies the number of tracks per side (1 to 999) for the logical drive (default: 80). Common entries are 80 (for 1.2Mb and 3.5-inch drives) and 40 (for 360Kb drives).

/S:*ss* specifies the number of sectors per track (1 to 40) for the logical drive (default: 9); 9, 15, and 18 are appropriate values.

/H:*hh* specifies the number of writing/reading heads (1 to 99). Floppy-disk drives normally have two heads.

/C specifies change-line support. The change line lets the CPU know if the disk-drive door is open.

/N labels a hard disk.

/F:*f* specifies the drive type (see Table 16.4). The default is 2.

| Drive Type | Drive Capacity |
|------------|----------------|
| 0 | 160Kb, 180Kb, 320Kb, 360Kb |
| 1 | 1.2Mb |
| 2 | 720Kb |
| 7 | 1.44Mb |

*Table 16.4: Drive types for the /F parameter*

In the following example, 360Kb drive—the second disk drive of an AT—is assigned the logical drive label B:

```
DEVICE=DRIVER.SYS /D:1 /T:40 /S:9 /H:2 /C
  /F:0
```

# PRINTER.SYS

PRINTER.SYS permits switching between code pages for the IBM Proprinter Model 4201 and the IBM Quietwriter III Model 5202. As with most device drivers, PRINTER.SYS must be executed in conjunction with the DEVICE command in the CONFIG.SYS file:

*Switching code pages*

```
PRINTER.SYS LPT x =(printertype [, [
   codepage] [, n] )
```

For the printer type, you can enter 4201 or 5202 for the IBM printers with those model numbers or for printers compatible with them. The code page is one of the character set tables 437, 850, 860, 863, or 865, and *n* specifies how many additional code pages can be addressed. This is one example of installing the driver:

```
DEVICE=C:\DOS\PRINTER.SYS LPT1:=(5202,
   437,850,2)
```

This device driver is useful only if you are using a printer that allows code-page switching.

# RAMDRIVE.SYS

MS-DOS comes with RAMDRIVE.SYS, and PC-DOS comes with VDISK.SYS. Both device drivers have the same syntax and work the same way. Creating RAM disks with VDISK.SYS is treated in detail in Step 18.

*RAM-DRIVE.SYS*

# VDISK.SYS

VDISK.SYS installs a virtual RAM disk to the standard or extended memory of a PC in addition to the existing physical drives. The creation of a RAM disk and the use of this disk are discussed in detail in Step 18.

*VDISK.SYS*

The layout of your keyboard is not permanent, and there are many ways to modify it. When you boot your computer, the American keyboard is assigned as default. You can change your keyboard layout by executing the KEYB command in your AUTOEXEC.BAT file.

*KEYB command*

The command

        KEYB GR

*Foreign keyboards*

reassigns the keyboard according to the German standard. Key assignments for other countries can also be set up with this command. You will find a list of possible settings in Table 17.1.

| *Country* | *Keyboard Code* |
|-----------|-----------------|
| Australia | US |
| Belgium | BE |
| Canada (English) | US |
| Canada (French) | CF |
| Denmark | DK |
| Germany | GR |
| Finland | SU |
| France | FR |
| Italy | IT |
| Latin America | LA |
| Netherlands | NL |

*Keyboard codes for KEYB*

*Table 17.1: Keyboard codes for KEYB*

| Country | Keyboard Code |
|---------|---------------|
| Norway | NO |
| Portugal | PO |
| Spain | SP |
| Sweden | SV |
| Switzerland (French) | SF |
| Switzerland (German) | SG |
| United Kingdom | UK |
| United States | US |

*Table 17.1: Keyboard codes for KEYB (cont.)*

All keyboard assignments have two limitations:

- Not every character can be displayed on the screen with one keystroke. Characters not shown on the keys (such as graphic and other special characters) can only be "conjured up" on the screen with an Alt-key combination.

- The function keys are only partially assigned (with editing functions). Sometimes it would be helpful if, instead of or in addition to these functions, pressing a function key would insert a frequently used DOS command or text (a long path, for example).

*ANSI.SYS*

You can assign any desired characters, even long character sequences such as DOS commands or text, to a chosen key by using the ANSI.SYS device driver and some programming work. One keystroke might then insert the command

```
DIR D:\WORD5\INVOICE\REMINDER\*.3ST
```

You can take advantage of the fourfold assignment of the function keys. Depending on your keyboard, 40 or 48 function-key assignments are available to you, so you will probably not need to reassign any of the typewriter keys. Create a template listing your function-key assignments that you can post in a visible spot near your workstation (see Figure 17.1).

Before you will be able to try the following examples and reassign your keyboard, the ANSI.SYS device drivers must be entered into your CONFIG.SYS file with the DEVICE command, and the system must be rebooted. Then you can use an escape sequence to reassign:

> `Esc[0;keycode; "reassignment"p`

Replace *keycode* with one of the codes from Table 17.2; *reassignment* is any character string that will be generated when the desired function key is pressed.

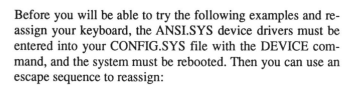

| Standard Commands | Data Backup | Programming | Paths |
|---|---|---|---|
| F1 | Shift-F1 | Ctrl-F1 | Alt-F1 |
| DIR | BACKUP C:\WORD\*.TXT A: | DEBUG | C:\WORD |
| F2 | Shift-F2 | Ctrl-F2 | Alt-F2 |
| DEL | BACKUP D:\GRAPHICS\*.* A: | EXE2BIN | D:\GRAPHICS |
| F3 | Shift-F3 | Ctrl-F3 | Alt-F3 |
| FORMAT A: | BACKUP D:\OFFICE\1\*.* A: | LINK | D:\OFFICE\1 |
| F4 | Shift-F4 | Ctrl-F4 | Alt-F4 |
| FORMAT A:/4 | BACKUP D:\OFFICE\2\*.* A: | EDLIN | D:\OFFICE\2 |
| F5 | Shift-F5 | Ctrl-F5 | Alt-F5 |
| DISKCOPY | BACKUP D:\OFFICE\3\*.* | MODE COM1:2400,e,8 | D:\OFFICE\3 |
| F6 | Shift-F6 | Ctrl-F6 | Alt-F6 |
| DISKCOMP | | MODE COM1:9600,e,8 | |
| F7 | Shift-F7 | Ctrl-F7 | Alt-F7 |
| DATE | | MODE LPT1:=COM2 | |
| F8 | Shift-F8 | Ctrl-F8 | Alt-F8 |
| TIME | | PROMPT $p$g | |
| F9 | Shift-F9 | Ctrl-F9 | Alt-F9 |
| LABEL | | | |
| F10 | Shift-F10 | Ctrl-F10 | Alt-F10 |
| F11 | Shift-F11 | Ctrl-F11 | Alt-F11 |
| F12 | Shift-F12 | Ctrl-F12 | Alt-F12 |

*Function-key template*

*Figure 17.1: Example of a template with function-key assignments*

*PROMPT command*

You should use the PROMPT command for entering, so replace *Esc* with *$e*:

```
PROMPT $e[0;59;"DIR";13p
```

You can enter this type of command at the DOS prompt. In this case, as in Figure 17.1, the DIR command is assigned to the F1 key. An Enter character (13) follows the DIR command, so that pressing the F1 key immediately displays the current directory contents.

*Keyboard codes*

| Function Key | Alone | With Shift | With Ctrl | With Alt |
| --- | --- | --- | --- | --- |
| F1 | 59 | 84 | 94 | 104 |
| F2 | 60 | 85 | 95 | 105 |
| F3 | 61 | 86 | 96 | 106 |
| F4 | 62 | 87 | 97 | 107 |
| F5 | 63 | 88 | 98 | 108 |
| F6 | 64 | 89 | 99 | 109 |
| F7 | 65 | 90 | 100 | 110 |
| F8 | 66 | 91 | 101 | 111 |
| F9 | 67 | 92 | 102 | 112 |
| F10 | 68 | 93 | 103 | 113 |
| F11 | 133* | 135* | 137* | 139* |
| F12 | 134* | 136* | 138* | 140* |

\*   *The function keys F11 and F12 are available only on some keyboards. The keyboard codes of F11 and F12 are not uniform. If you do not find the corresponding codes for your keyboard in the manual, simply experiment with different numbers.*

*Table 17.2: The expanded keyboard codes of the function keys*

You can also place the DIR command in the AUTOEXEC.BAT file (or another batch file). ECHO must be switched on when the command is used in a batch file, otherwise the escape sequence will not be output. After execution of the batch file, the word *PROMPT* will appear, followed by several blank lines.

Since entering this command erases the DOS prompt, you will have to reset it:

*Reset prompt*

```
PROMPT $P$G
```

You can write the escape sequence to a text file with EDLIN and then display it with the TYPE command:

*Escape sequence with a text file*

```
C:\>EDLIN F3.DAT <Enter>
*i<Enter>
    1:*<Ctrl><V>[[0;61;"FORMAT A:";13p
      <Enter>
    2:*<Ctrl><C>
*e<Enter>
C:\>TYPE F3.DAT <Enter>
```

*F3.DAT*

This example shows all the keystrokes you will need to enter as well as DOS and EDLIN prompts. Do not enter the characters contained within the angle brackets—just press the corresponding key. The F3.DAT file contains the escape sequence for assigning the FORMAT command to the F3 key. The escape character in this case has been replaced by the Ctrl-V key combination and the bracket. ^V[ will appear on the screen at this point. If you were now to edit the line, you would find that the ^V[ character sequence is automatically replaced by ^[ (the character for Esc). The TYPE command for this file would display four blank lines. Pressing the F3

*Escape
sequence
with
ECHO*

key, though, will verify that the key has been reassigned.
The escape sequence used with ECHO is displayed in a similar manner:

```
C:\>EDLIN F3.BAT <Enter>
*i   <Enter>
  1:*ECHO <Ctrl><V>[[0;61;"FORMAT A:";
        13p   <Enter>
  2:*<Ctrl><C>
*e   <Enter>
C:\>F3   <Enter>
```

# Step 18
# RAM Disk

In this step, you will learn how a virtual drive is installed in memory (RAM) in addition to the available physical drives (floppy disk, hard disk). This simulated drive is called a *RAM disk*.

*RAM disk*

The speed at which you can write to a RAM disk or read data from it is relative to the speed of your memory and therefore lies in the nanosecond range (60 to 120 ns, where 1 ns equals $1 \times 10^{-9}$s or 0.000000001 s). In comparison, accessing a hard disk, even with the faster disks, is significantly slower (<20 ms, where 1 ms = 1 x $10^{-3}$s or 0.001 s).

*Access speed*

Since a RAM disk is created in memory, its contents are lost when you switch off the computer or experience a power failure. The contents of a RAM disk must always be saved before you switch off the computer. The only exception to this is the RAM disk on some laptops or other computers whose standard memory is backed up with a battery.

Unless your computer has more than 640Kb memory, it is hardly worth your trouble to install a RAM disk. There will be no great advantages in terms of speed unless the computer has 1Mb of memory, and memory space beyond the first 640Kb can be used for the RAM disk.

*Size of memory*

A RAM disk is created by means of the device driver VDISK.SYS (with PC-DOS; or RAMDRIVE with MS-DOS):

*Creating a RAM disk*

```
DEVICE=VDISK.SYS  [size][sector-size]
    [number-entries][/E[:n]
```

*Comments*

You can include a comment for each parameter (except the switch /E). The following entry is also possible:

```
DEVICE=VDISK.SYS disksize=[size] sector-
    size=[sector-size] directory-entry=
    [number-entries] [/E[:n]]
```

*Size parameter*

The entry with the DEVICE command must be placed in the CONFIG.SYS file. The memory capacity of the RAM disk is established by the *size* parameter. If there is a size specification, DOS automatically creates a 64Kb RAM disk.

*Sector size parameter*

The *sector-size* parameter determines the minimum memory space for one file. The larger this value, the faster the access to the RAM disk is. The default value is 128, and the value can be increased to 256 or 512.

*Number of entries parameter*

The *number-entries* parameter determines the maximum number of directories and files that you can enter into one directory of a RAM disk. Values can range from 2 to 512; the default is 64.

*Extended memory*

If you have more than 640Kb of standard memory available and this can be addressed as extended memory, you can create the RAM disk in extended memory with /E. You can also specify how many sectors will be exchanged simultaneously between base memory and extended memory. This default is 8 sectors, and ordinarily does not need to be changed.

The following command creates a RAM disk of 256Kb in the extended memory:

*Example*

```
DEVICE=C:\DOS\VDISK.SYS disk-size=256
    sector-size=128 directory-entries=128 /E
```

*Drive label*

Each sector of this RAM disk is 128 bytes in size, and a maximum of 128 files or directories can be written to it. Upon access, 8 sectors can be directly read from or written to (default setting). If you have installed a hard disk with the label C and a floppy-disk drive with the label A and have no other drive, the letter D (the next available letter) will be assigned as the drive letter for the RAM disk.

If you have a system with five or more drives, the labels A to F provided by the system are occupied. In this case, a new drive label must be reserved with the LASTDRIVE command:

```
LASTDRIVE=G
```

The LASTDRIVE command, like the DEVICE command, is written into the CONFIG.SYS file. It must precede the DEVICE command.

Once the RAM disk is installed, you can store frequently used programs and files on it. From time to time (approximately every 30 minutes), you should save your data files to a floppy or hard disk to prevent losing a large amount of work should your system lock or should you experience a power failure. It is a good idea to write the necessary copy commands to the AUTOEXEC.BAT file, so that files will be automatically copied to your RAM disk once you have created it.

You should also copy frequently used DOS commands such as CHKDSK, XCOPY, or EDLIN onto the RAM disk. If you adjust the setting of COMSPEC accordingly, you can even copy COMMAND.COM to the RAM disk.

*Optimiza-
tion*

```
COPY C:\COMMAND.COM D:
SET COMPSPEC=D:\COMMAND.COM
```

The DEBUG program is not mentioned in DOS 3.3 manuals, since using it incorrectly could lead quickly to the loss of data or to unintentional changes in application programs. However, each user should decide whether to use DEBUG. If your computer locks while you experiment with DEBUG, simply reboot it.

DEBUG is a debugger—that is, a program a programmer uses to search for errors. Programmers also use DEBUG to enter assembler commands that DEBUG converts into machine language and then executes in this language. Conversely, EXE or COM programs can be disassembled—DEBUG converts machine-language programs into a form of assembly source code that trained individuals can read. The assembly source code that DEBUG produces is not suitable for an assembler, such as Microsoft MASM or Borland TASM, to read and convert back into machine language.

*Debugger*

*Assembler*

*Dis-assembler*

Experienced users will ordinarily use DEBUG to modify an EXE or COM program according to certain instructions (for example, to patch a game) or to search for and replace control characters or locators in data files. If you use an XT, you can initialize a hard disk with DEBUG.

*Patches*

You execute DEBUG by entering the program name, optionally followed by name of the file that will be examined or modified with DEBUG:

*Executing DEBUG*

    [d:path] DEBUG [filespec] [parameter...]

You can specify optional parameters if these are necessary to run the specified program file.

| | |
|---|---|
| *Prompt* | When you execute DEBUG, only a hyphen will appear; this is the DEBUG prompt. Entering a question mark or pressing the F1 key has no effect—there are no auxiliary functions. You will find all DEBUG commands in Table 19.1 at the end of this step. |
| *Initializing a hard disk* | The following example shows how the hard disk of an XT can be initialized with DEBUG. This procedure cannot be used on an AT, because AT hard disks must be formatted with the program they come with. Be aware that when you format a hard disk, all data on it is erased (including the partition division). |

Execute the debugger to initialize the hard disk:

    DEBUG

Next, enter the RAX command:

| | |
|---|---|
| *R command* |     **-RAX** |

After DEBUG responds with a colon, specify the drive number and the interleave factor:

    0005

| | |
|---|---|
| *Deter-mining interleave factor* | In this example, the drive is C (00). The drive can be labeled from 0 to 7. The interleave factor is 5 (05). You can use this value for an XT hard disk. After installation, you can determine the optimum interleave factor with a test program such as SpinRite II, then repeat the formatting. |

Be sure to follow the instructions that come with the PC or controller. Entering an invalid command can cause chaos.

You can now start the formatting program. Generally, the start address is C800:5:

| | |
|---|---|
| *G command* |     **G=C800:5** |

Some formatting programs prompt you for initializing parameters. If this happens, you can execute the program directly with the G command. This way, you avoid using the R command to enter the drive specification and interleave factors in the AX register.

You will now learn about patching a program using the EXE2BIN command as an example. EXE2BIN is a program used to convert EXE files into COM files and was a component of DOS through MS/PC-DOS version 3.2. Beginning with MS/PC-DOS 3.3, this program is no longer being supplied. You cannot use the EXE2BIN program of an older DOS version without modification, since this program queries for the current DOS version. The result of the internal test is 0 if the DOS version agrees with the version of the program. A conditional jump command at offset 30D (JZ=jump on zero) jumps to the actual beginning of the program. Through DEBUG, this command can be changed to an unconditional jump command:

*Patching EXE2BIN*

```
DEBUG
-E 30D EB
-W
-Q
```

You can execute the patching according to instructions in magazines or books. To understand these instructions, however, you will need a thorough knowledge of machine language for the 8088/86 or one of its successors (80286, 80386), a knowledge of systems and hardware, and a lot of practice. A overview of the commands available when using DEBUG is found in Table 19.1.

| Command | Description |
|---------|-------------|
| A [*address*] | Assembles instructions following the current or specified address. |
| C *area address* | Compares two memory blocks. |
| D [*address*][*address\length*] | Displays memory contents. |
| E *address* [*list*] | Changes information stored following the specified address. |
| F *area list* | Fills the specified memory area with values from the list. |
| G [=*address*][*address*[*address*...]] | Executes program in memory following the specified address. |
| H *value1 value2* | Performs calculations with hex values. |
| I *port-address* | Reads a single byte from a port. |
| L [*address*[*drive sector sector*] | Loads a file from an address or a specified floppy-disk/hard-disk area. |
| M *area address* | Moves the memory area to the specified address. |

*Table 19.1: List of DEBUG commands*

| | |
|---|---|
| N *filespec* | Specifies a file name in preparation for writing or reading a file. |
| O *port address byte* | Transmits a single byte to the specified port. |
| P [=*address*][*value*] | Executes a loop or subroutine. |
| Q | Terminates DEBUG without saving. |
| R [*register*] | Displays or modifies contents of registers. |
| S *register list* | Searches for the characters of the list in the specified area. |
| T [=*address*][*value*] | Executes the program by steps and displays the contents of register and flags. |
| U [*address/area*] | Disassembles the commands in the specified area. |
| W [*address*[*drive sect sect sect*]] | Writes data at the specified location on the floppy disk/hard disk. |

*Table 19.1: List of DEBUG commands (cont.)*

# Step 20
# DOS Utilities

You have probably already recognized the limits of some of the DOS commands. The DIR command, for example, cannot display files with the hidden file attribute, and the BACKUP and RESTORE commands are useful only if you have a lot of time. And working with DOS involves many complicated commands.

Thousands of utility programs are offered that make operating your computer easier and offer additional functions. A few representative programs are introduced here.

## Online Help

MS/PC-DOS 3.3 does not provide any help at the DOS prompt. You must look up or tediously memorize the required commands. With the DOS Online Advisor, you can get online help for the DOS program. Once the DOS Online Advisor is installed, you need only press a hotkey to see the online help on your screen. You can cross-reference related topics with pull-down menus. This utility indexes 2300 DOS topics and covers 200 DOS error messages.

*DOS Online Advisor*

DOS Online Advisor is available from:

SYBAR Software
c/o SYBEX Inc.
2021 Challenger Drive
Alameda, CA 94501
(800) 227–2346

## Easier PC Operation

Managing multiple directories with thousands of files can quickly become a tedious operation using DOS alone.

*QDOS II*

QDOS II is among the utility programs available that display the directory structure and offer a selection of file management functions such as deleting, copying, moving multiple files, making and removing subdirectories, and so on.

QDOS II is available from:

Gazelle Systems
42 N. University Ave., Suite 10
Provo, UT  84601
(800) 233–0383

## Data Recovery

*The Norton Utilities*

With The Norton Utilities, you can recover deleted files and even retrieve or recover data from formatted hard disks. There are also programs offering an abundance of additional functions.

You can obtain information on The Norton Utilities from:

Peter Norton Computing
100 Wilshire Blvd., 9th floor
Santa Monica, CA  90401
(213) 319–2010

## Data Backup

*Fastback Plus*

The limitations of DOS become particularly clear when you attempt to back up a hard disk of 40Mb or more with BACKUP. Data backup becomes an exhausting job that takes hours. It can be done much more simply: using a program such as Fastback Plus, it takes about a half-hour to back up a 40Mb hard disk. Under certain conditions, you will only need half as many floppy disks as with BACKUP.

You can obtain information on Fastback Plus from:

Fifth Generation Systems
10049 N. Reiger Rd.
Baton Rouge, LA 70809
(800) 873–4384

## Maintaining the Hard Disk

Disk Technician is a noteworthy product that every hard-disk owner will find useful. It is simple, but it does something that DOS ignores: it corrects data errors and regulates data maintenance on your hard disk.

*Disk Technician*

You can obtain information on Disk Technician from:

Prime Solutions, Inc.
1940 Garnet Ave.
San Diego, CA 92109
(619) 274–5000

## Fragmentation

Fragmentation of files on a hard disk causes a significant slowing down of hard-disk access. The Disk Optimizer program reorganizes the hard disk so that previously fragmented files are stored in consecutive blocks (clusters), thereby speeding up disk access.

*Disk Optimizer*

You can obtain information on the Disk Optimizer from:

SoftLogic Solutions
1 Perimeter Rd.
Manchester, NH 03103
(603) 644–5555

# Index

# Selections from The SYBEX Library

## OPERATING SYSTEMS

### The ABC's of DOS 4
**Alan R. Miller**
275pp. Ref. 583-2
This step-by-step introduction to using DOS 4 is written especially for beginners. Filled with simple examples, *The ABC's of DOS 4* covers the basics of hardware, software, disks, the system editor EDLIN, DOS commands, and more.

### ABC's of MS-DOS (Second Edition)
**Alan R. Miller**
233pp. Ref. 493-3
This handy guide to MS-DOS is all many PC users need to manage their computer files, organize floppy and hard disks, use EDLIN, and keep their computers organized. Additional information is given about utilities like Sidekick, and there is a DOS command and program summary. The second edition is fully updated for Version 3.3.

### DOS Assembly Language Programming
**Alan R. Miller**
365pp. 487-9
This book covers PC-DOS through 3.3, and gives clear explanations of how to assemble, link, and debug 8086, 8088, 80286, and 80386 programs. The example assembly language routines are valuable for students and programmers alike.

### DOS Instant Reference
**SYBEX Prompter Series**
**Greg Harvey**
**Kay Yarborough Nelson**
220pp. Ref. 477-1, 4 ¾" × 8"
A complete fingertip reference for fast, easy

on-line help:command summaries, syntax, usage and error messages. Organized by function—system commands, file commands, disk management, directories, batch files, I/O, networking, programming, and more. Through Version 3.3.

### DOS User's Desktop Companion
**SYBEX Ready Reference Series**
**Judd Robbins**
969pp. Ref. 505-0
This comprehensive reference covers DOS commands, batch files, memory enhancements, printing, communications and more information on optimizing each user's DOS environment. Written with step-by-step instructions and plenty of examples, this volume covers all versions through 3.3.

### Encyclopedia DOS
**Judd Robbins**
1030pp. Ref. 699-5
A comprehensive reference and user's guide to all versions of DOS through 4.0. Offers complete information on every DOS command, with all possible switches and parameters -- plus examples of effective usage. An invaluable tool.

### Essential OS/2 (Second Edition)
**Judd Robbins**
445pp. Ref. 609-X
Written by an OS/2 expert, this is the guide to the powerful new resources of the OS/2 operating system standard edition 1.1 with presentation manager. Robbins introduces the standard edition, and details multitasking under OS/2, and the range of commands for installing, starting up, configuring, and running applications. For Version 1.1 Standard Edition.

## Essential PC-DOS
## (Second Edition)
**Myril Clement Shaw**
**Susan Soltis Shaw**
332pp. Ref. 413-5
An authoritative guide to PC-DOS, including version 3.2. Designed to make experts out of beginners, it explores everything from disk management to batch file programming. Includes an 85-page command summary. Through Version 3.2.

## Graphics Programming
## Under Windows
**Brian Myers**
**Chris Doner**
646pp. Ref. 448-8
Straightforward discussion, abundant examples, and a concise reference guide to graphics commands make this book a must for Windows programmers. Topics range from how Windows works to programming for business, animation, CAD, and desktop publishing. For Version 2.

## Hard Disk Instant Reference
## SYBEX Prompter Series
**Judd Robbins**
256pp. Ref. 587-5, 4 ¾" × 8"
Compact yet comprehensive, this pocket-sized reference presents the essential information on DOS commands used in managing directories and files, and in optimizing disk configuration. Includes a survey of third-party utility capabilities. Through DOS 4.0.

## The IBM PC-DOS Handbook
## (Third Edition)
**Richard Allen King**
359pp. Ref. 512-3
A guide to the inner workings of PC-DOS 3.2, for intermediate to advanced users and programmers of the IBM PC series. Topics include disk, screen and port control, batch files, networks, compatibility, and more. Through Version 3.3.

## Inside DOS: A Programmer's
## Guide
**Michael J. Young**
490pp. Ref. 710-X

A collection of practical techniques (with source code listings) designed to help you take advantage of the rich resources intrinsic to MS-DOS machines. Designed for the experienced programmer with a basic understanding of C and 8086 assembly language, and DOS fundamentals.

## Mastering DOS
## (Second Edition)
**Judd Robbins**
722pp. Ref. 555-7
"The most useful DOS book." This seven-part, in-depth tutorial addresses the needs of users at all levels. Topics range from running applications, to managing files and directories, configuring the system, batch file programming, and techniques for system developers. Through Version 4.

## MS-DOS Advanced
## Programming
**Michael J. Young**
490pp. Ref. 578-6
Practical techniques for maximizing performance in MS-DOS software by making best use of system resources. Topics include functions, interrupts, devices, multitasking, memory residency and more, with examples in C and assembler. Through Version 3.3.

## MS-DOS Handbook
## (Third Edition)
**Richard Allen King**
362pp. Ref. 492-5
This classic has been fully expanded and revised to include the latest features of MS-DOS Version 3.3. Two reference books in one, this title has separate sections for programmer and user. Multi-DOS partitons, 3 ½-inch disk format, batch file call and return feature, and comprehensive coverage of MS-DOS commands are included. Through Version 3.3.

## MS-DOS Power User's Guide,
## Volume I
## (Second Edition)
**Jonathan Kamin**
482pp. Ref. 473-9

A fully revised, expanded edition of our best-selling guide to high-performance DOS techniques and utilities—with details on Version 3.3. Configuration, I/O, directory structures, hard disks, RAM disks, batch file programming, the ANSI.SYS device driver, more. Through Version 3.3.

## Programmers Guide to the OS/2 Presentation Manager
**Michael J. Young**
683pp. Ref. 569-7
This is the definitive tutorial guide to writing programs for the OS/2 Presentation Manager. Young starts with basic architecture, and explores every important feature including scroll bars, keyboard and mouse interface, menus and accelerators, dialogue boxes, clipboards, multitasking, and much more.

## Programmer's Guide to Windows (Second Edition)
**David Durant**
**Geta Carlson**
**Paul Yao**
704pp. Ref. 496-8
The first edition of this programmer's guide was hailed as a classic. This new edition covers Windows 2 and Windows/386 in depth. Special emphasis is given to over fifty new routines to the Windows interface, and to preparation for OS/2 Presentation Manager compatibility.

## Understanding DOS 3.3
**Judd Robbins**
678pp. Ref. 648-0
This best selling, in-depth tutorial addresses the needs of users at all levels with many examples and hands-on exercises. Robbins discusses the fundamentals of DOS, then covers manipulating files and directories, using the DOS editor, printing, communicating, and finishes with a full section on batch files.

## Understanding Hard Disk Management on the PC
**Jonathan Kamin**
500pp. Ref. 561-1
This title is a key productivity tool for all

hard disk users who want efficient, error-free file management and organization. Includes details on the best ways to conserve hard disk space when using several memory-guzzling programs. Through DOS 4.

## Up & Running with Your Hard Disk
**Klaus M Rubsam**
140pp. Ref. 666-9
A far-sighted, compact introduction to hard disk installation and basic DOS use. Perfect for PC users who want the practical essentials in the shortest possible time. In 20 basic steps, learn to choose your hard disk, work with accessories, back up data, use DOS utilities to save time, and more.

## Up & Running with Windows 286/386
**Gabriele Wentges**
132pp. Ref. 691-X
This handy 20-step overview gives PC users all the essentials of using Windows - - whether for evaluating the software, or getting a fast start. Each self-contained lesson takes just 15 minutes to one hour to complete.

# COMMUNICATIONS

## Mastering Crosstalk XVI (Second Edition)
**Peter W. Gofton**
225pp. Ref. 642-1
Introducing the communications program Crosstalk XVI for the IBM PC. As well as providing extensive examples of command and script files for programming Crosstalk, this book includes a detailed description of how to use the program's more advanced features, such as windows, talking to mini or mainframe, customizing the keyboard and answering calls and background mode.

## Mastering PROCOMM PLUS
**Bob Campbell**
400pp. Ref. 657-X
Learn all about communications and information retrieval as you master and use PROCOMM PLUS. Topics include choosing and using a modem; automatic dialing; using on-line services (featuring CompuServe) and more. Through Version 1.1b; also covers PROCOMM, the "shareware" version.

## Mastering Serial Communications
**Peter W. Gofton**
289pp. Ref. 180-2
The software side of communications, with details on the IBM PC's serial programming, the XMODEM and Kermit protocols, non-ASCII data transfer, interrupt-level programming and more. Sample programs in C, assembly language and BASIC.

# NETWORKS

## The ABC's of Local Area Networks
**Michael Dortch**
212pp. Ref. 664-2
This jargon-free introduction to LANs is fur current and prospective users who see general information, comparative options, a look at the future, and tips for effective LANs use today. With comparisons of Token-Ring, PC Network, Novell, and others.

## The ABC's of Novell Netware
**Jeff Woodward**
282pp. Ref. 614-6
For users who are new to PC's or networks, this entry-level tutorial outlines each basic element and operation of Novell. The ABC's introduces computer hardware and software, DOS, network organization and security, and printing and communicating over the netware system.

## Mastering Novell Netware
**Cheryl C. Currid**
**Craig A. Gillett**
500pp. Ref. 630-8
This book is a thorough guide for System Administrators to installing and operating a microcomputer network using Novell Netware. Mastering covers actually setting up a network from start to finish, design, administration, maintenance, and troubleshooting.

## Networking with TOPS
**Steven William Rimmer**
350pp. Ref. 565-4
A hands on guide to the most popular user friendly network available. This book will walk a user through setting up the hardware and software of a variety of TOPS configurations, from simple two station networks through whole offices. It explains the realities of sharing files between PC compatibles and Macintoshes, of sharing printers and other peripherals and, most important, of the real world performance one can expect when the network is running.

# UTILITIES

## Mastering the Norton Utilities
**Peter Dyson**
373pp. Ref. 575-1
In-depth descriptions of each Norton utility make this book invaluable for beginning and experienced users alike. Each utility is described clearly with examples and the text is organized so that readers can put Norton to work right away. Version 4.5.

## Mastering PC Tools Deluxe
**Peter Dyson**
400pp. Ref. 654-5
A complete hands-on guide to the timesaving—and "lifesaving"—utility programs in Version 5.5 of PC Tools Deluxe. Contains concise tutorials and in-depth discussion of every aspect of using PC Tools—from high speed backups, to data recovery, to using Desktop applications.

## Mastering SideKick Plus
**Gene Weisskopf**
394pp. Ref. 558-1
Employ all of Sidekick's powerful and expanded features with this hands-on guide to the popular utility. Features include comprehensive and detailed coverage of time management, note taking, outlining, auto dialing, DOS file management, math, and copy-and-paste functions.

## Up & Running with Norton Utilities
**Rainer Bartel**
140pp. Ref. 659-6
Get up and running in the shortest possible time in just 20 lessons or "steps." Learn to restore disks and files, use UnErase, edit your floppy disks, retrieve lost data and more. Or use the book to evaluate the software before you purchase. Through Version 4.2.

## Up & Running with PC Tools Deluxe 6
**Thomas Holste**
180pp. Ref.678-2
Learn to use this software program in just 20 basic steps. Readers get a quick, inexpensive introduction to using the Tools for disaster recovery, disk and file management, and more.

# HARDWARE

## From Chips to Systems: An Introduction to Microcomputers (Second Edition)
**Rodnay Zaks**
**Alexander Wolfe**
580pp. Ref. 377-5
The best-selling introduction to microcomputer hardware—now fully updated, revised, and illustrated. Such recent advances as 32-bit processors and RISC architecture are introduced and explained for the first time in a beginning text.

## Microprocessor Interfacing Techniques (Third Edition)
**Austin Lesea**
**Rodnay Zaks**
456pp. Ref. 029-6
This handbook is for engineers and hobbyists alike, covering every aspect of interfacing microprocessors with peripheral devices. Topics include assembling a CPU, basic I/O, analog circuitry, and bus standards.

## The RS-232 Solution (Second Edition)
**Joe Campbell**
193pp. Ref. 488-7
For anyone wanting to use their computer's serial port, this complete how-to guide is updated and expanded for trouble-free RS-232-C interfacing from scratch. Solution shows you how to connect a variety of computers, printers, and modems, and it includes details for IBM PC AT, PS/2, and Macintosh.

# DATABASES

## The ABC's of dBASE III PLUS
**Robert Cowart**
264pp. Ref. 379-1
The most efficient way to get beginners up and running with dBASE. Every 'how' and 'why' of database management is demonstrated through tutorials and practical dBASE III PLUS applications.

## The ABC's of dBASE IV
**Robert Cowart**
338pp. Ref. 531-X
This superb tutorial introduces beginners to the concept of databases and practical dBASE IV applications featuring the new menu-driven interface, the new report writer, and Query by Example.

## The ABC's of Paradox
**Charles Siegel**
300pp. Ref. 573-5

Easy to understand and use, this introduction is written so that the computer novice can create, edit, and manage complex Paradox databases. This primer is filled with examples of the Paradox 3.0 menu structure.

## Advanced Techniques in dBASE III PLUS
**Alan Simpson**
454pp. Ref. 369-4
A full course in database design and structured programming, with routines for inventory control, accounts receivable, system management, and integrated databases.

## dBASE Instant Reference
### SYBEX Prompter Series
**Alan Simpson**
471pp. Ref. 484-4; 4 3/4" × 8"
Comprehensive information at a glance: a brief explanation of syntax and usage for every dBASE command, with step-by-step instructions and exact keystroke sequences. Commands are grouped by function in twenty precise categories.

## dBASE III PLUS Programmer's Reference Guide
### SYBEX Ready Reference Series
**Alan Simpson**
1056pp. Ref. 508-5
Programmers will save untold hours and effort using this comprehensive, well-organized dBASE encyclopedia. Complete technical details on commands and functions, plus scores of often-needed algorithms.

## dBASE IV Programmer's Instant Reference
### SYBEX Prompter Series
**Alan Simpson**
544pp. Ref. 538-7, 4 3/4" × 8"
This comprehensive reference to every dBASE command and function has everything for the dBASE programmer in a compact, pocket-sized book. Fast and easy access to adding data, sorting, performing calculations, managing multiple databases, memory variables and arrays,

windows and menus, networking, and much more. Version 1.1.

## dBASE IV User's Desktop Companion
### SYBEX Ready Reference Series
**Alan Simpson**
950pp. Ref. 523-9
This easy-to-use reference provides an exhaustive resource guide to taking full advantage of the powerful non-programming features of the dBASE IV Control Center. This book discusses query by example, custom reports and data entry screens, macros, the application generator, and the dBASE command and programming language.

## dBASE IV User's Instant Reference
### SYBEX Prompter Series
**Alan Simpson**
349pp. Ref. 605-7, 4 3/4" × 8"
This handy pocket-sized reference book gives every new dBASE IV user fast and easy access to any dBASE command. Arranged alphabetically and by function, each entry includes a description, exact syntax, an example, and special tips from Alan Simpson.

## Mastering dBASE III PLUS: A Structured Approach
**Carl Townsend**
342pp. Ref. 372-4
In-depth treatment of structured programming for custom dBASE solutions. An ideal study and reference guide for applications developers, new and experienced users with an interest in efficient programming.

## Mastering Paradox (Fourth Edition)
**Alan Simpson**
636pp. Ref. 612-X
Best selling author Alan Simpson simplifies all aspects of Paradox for the beginning to intermediate user. The book starts with database basics, covers multiple tables, graphics, custom applications with PAL, and the Personal Programmer. For Version 3.0.